Men and the Art of
MARRIAGE MAINTENANCE

Men and the Art of
MARRIAGE MAINTENANCE

By Brett C. McInelly

Horizon Publishers
Springville, Utah

ISBN 13: 978-0-88290-807-3
ISBN 10: 0-88290-807-3

Published by CFI, an imprint of Cedar Fort, Inc., 925 N. Main, Springville, UT, 84663
Distributed by Cedar Fort, Inc. www.cedarfort.com

LIBRARY OF CONGRESS CATALOGING-IN-PUBLICATION DATA

McInelly, Brett C.
   Men and the art of marriage maintenance / by Brett C. McInelly. -- 1st ed.
      p. cm.
   ISBN 0-88290-807-3
   1. Marriage--Religious aspects--Mormon Church. 2. Men--Psychology. 3. Church of Jesus Christ of Latter-day Saints--Doctrines 4. Mormon Church--Doctrines. I. Title.

   BX8641.M35 2006
   248.8'425--dc22

                                          2006019998

Cover design by Nicole Williams
Cover design © 2006 by Lyle Mortimer
Printed in the United States of America

10   9   8   7   6   5   4   3   2   1

Printed on acid-free paper

Dedication

For Kristin, my conscience, my muse, my love

Table of Contents

Introduction

In all fairness, I should start with a disclaimer.

I'm no expert. I'm not a marriage counselor. I do have a Ph.D., but it's in English literature, not psychology. And I'm not a perfect husband; in fact, some days I'm not even a very good one. I'd be the first to admit that, in many ways, I'm utterly unqualified to write a book about men and marriage.

Yet I've done exactly that. Why? First and foremost, I want nothing more than to be an outstanding husband and have a great marriage. I believe that most married men want these same things. For all the wisecracks we make about marriage while in the company of other men, and despite our frequent bouts with insensitivity, we really want to have exceptional marriages. Our motives, I'll admit, are partly selfish. We recognize that a good marriage generally leads to more and frequent golf outings, more and frequent intimate moments, and inner peace and serenity. Much of our mental and emotional health hinges on the state of our marriages.

But our motives aren't entirely self-centered. I think most of us want to be better husbands for our wives' sakes as well as our own. The ultimate payoff isn't the more and frequent golf, or even the more and frequent intimate moments. No, promoting our wives' happiness is its own reward; the other stuff is icing on the cake.

While perusing the pages of this book, you may get the impression that all I really care about is the icing. I won't lie. I love icing. I can't bear the thought of a world without icing. For me, marriage will always be partly about the icing. But I've learned that the icing is infinitely sweeter when I'm more concerned about my wife and her happiness than the icing. The less I focus on the icing and the more on her, the more I come to realize that the icing takes care of itself. In the end, I prefer cake; the icing is a mere complement, and the two definitely enhance the other.

No, I'm not an expert. But I am a man who earnestly strives to improve the quality of my marriage, occasionally experiencing success, occasionally enduring failure, and ultimately having a sense of awe at the wonders and mysteries of married life.

I should also mention that two assumptions underlie *Men and the Art of Marriage Maintenance*. One I've already identified—that most men genuinely want to improve their marriages. Second, these same men are often at a loss of how to do this. I hope the following chapters will provide these men with some direction as they explore with me some of the ins and outs of married life.

To my female readers, much of what I have to say regarding

the male psyche may come as no surprise. On the other hand, the following pages might help you better understand that creature you call husband.

To both my male and female readers, I hope the book makes you smile, perhaps even laugh. Laughter is, after all, an inherent part of joy, and joy is what marriage is ultimately all about.

one

How Taco Salad Wrecked an Otherwise Perfect Marriage:

Cook a Meal Together

The honeymoon for my wife and me ended over taco salad.

After a month of marital heaven, I was feeling extremely confident about the success of our marriage. We had been married a whole month, and I could see no signs of domestic strife. I was happy. My wife was happy. The worst part of the day was parting company in the morning as we each went off to our respective jobs. The best part was coming home and, of course, the constant hanky-panky. The slightest innuendo would lift the anchor, unfurl the sails, and set the ship on course. One morning I discovered the letters L-O-V-E in my bowl of Alphabets cereal. I pointed them out to my wife and, without a word, we were taking the bowl's advice. But all this ended over taco salad.

Not that there isn't anything exciting about taco salad. Give me a few pitted olives, some pinto beans, and a little spicy salsa, and I've got the makings of a fine romantic dinner. But the first time my wife and I made taco salad together proved to be an antidote to even the most potent love potion. As silly as it sounds, we found ourselves fighting for the first time in our married lives, all because we decided to make taco salad together.

As we grated cheese, sliced tomatoes and onions, and browned the hamburger, I took out several small bowls, in which I placed the aforementioned items. I was planning a taco salad bar. My wife, on the other hand, began dumping all the ingredients I had put into small bowls into one large bowl.

Baffled, I asked, "What are you doing?"

"Making taco salad," came the reply. "What are you doing?"

"Making taco salad," I said.

We each stood motionless for a moment trying to decipher the cryptic behavior of the other.

And then my wife committed the act that rocked the foundation of our heretofore blissful marriage. Before I could say a word, she began spooning mayonnaise into the browned ground beef!

"What are you doing now?" I screamed.

I couldn't believe my eyes. She was ruining the meat. Mayonnaise in taco salad? It didn't make sense. And my wife was equally dumbfounded. Why had I flipped a tortilla over a little mayonnaise?

Clearly, she had no clue how to make taco salad, so I felt compelled to explain the procedure. In a nutshell, you prepare the ingredients and put them in separate bowls. Then you assemble a taco salad to your own taste; and there's no place for mayonnaise in taco salad! It seemed so simple, so logical. Then came the revelation: there was another way to make taco salad. But who makes taco salad by dumping all the ingredients into one bowl and mixing mayonnaise into the meat? Clearly, my wife wasn't American. She is part Norwegian, so I assumed this must be the way they make taco salad in Norway. I quickly ascertained that I would have to set her straight or be reduced to eating Norwegian-style taco salad for the rest of my married life.

If I logically explained the merits of my version, I thought, surely she would see the light. But I soon learned that she was as firmly committed to her version of taco salad as I was to mine. The more I talked, the more she looked at me like I was a dumb gringo unaware of the nuances of fine Mexican cuisine. Within minutes, we were screaming at each other, and I could feel the constant hanky-panky slipping away.

It was time for a quick gut check. Was I so committed to my version of taco salad that I was willing to sacrifice the joys of conjugal relations? Certainly not, so I naturally deferred to my wife's method of making taco salad and to this day, we've never made it any other way. This can be partly attributed to my desire for marital bliss and partly to the fact that, as it turned out, her version of taco salad is delicious.

The moral of the story is not, as you may suspect, to avoid sharing the kitchen with your wife. Quite the contrary. Cooking with your wife can be a real pleasure. But when disagreements arise over what to put in the pot, I strongly suggest deferring to your wife's judgment.

The moral of the story is—and here comes a shocker—differences exist in marriage. Really. I've come to this weighty conclusion only after reflecting for years on the complexities of taco salad. I now realize that my wife and I weren't necessarily fighting about taco salad. We were fighting over two competing points of view, two different ways of doing things. We both were so uncompromisingly committed to our own style of taco salad that we failed to even consider the merits of the other's version.

We've experienced the same kind of tension when deciding on the best way to discipline our children or choosing the color of carpet for the living room floor. Inevitably, we both bring something different to the table, both literally and figuratively. More often than not, my wife demonstrates how my opinion or point of view is inherently flawed, but I still cling to the idea that one way of seeing or doing things isn't necessarily better than the other. They're just different, and working through these differences is part of what marriage is all about.

And cooking together may be a place to work through some of these differences. Find a recipe that is new to you and your wife, buy all the ingredients, and surprise her when you come home from work (with groceries in tow) by suggesting that the two of you cook dinner together. Of course, you can offer to prepare the meal on your own, but I suspect that both of you will have more fun cooking together. Just promise that you'll do the dishes afterward.

two

What Monkeys and Newly Married Men Have in Common:
Subtle Displays of Love

A recent trip to a family reunion confirmed what I believe to be a universal truth: new husbands are like monkeys.

At the reunion, I encountered a younger cousin and his new bride. They had been married only a week before and literally were en route from their honeymoon. Still reveling in each other and the joys of the previous week, they seemed oblivious to the realities of married life. Sure, they had been told marriage is hard, but they didn't believe it. So far, marriage for them had been a snap, a piece of cake. They were the exception to the rule. You could read it in their eyes, in the fact that they were connected at the hip by an invisible cord.

More experienced couples, particularly women, looked on with a hint of envy and a bit of a smirk. On one hand, we all wished we could return to that moment between exchanging vows and the first knock-down-drag-out fight when we deluded ourselves into believing that marriage was as easy as falling in love. On the other hand, we all knew the reality that awaited the happy couple and we couldn't help but think to ourselves, "If they only knew."

As I watched, I was particularly struck by the sharp contrast between my cousin's behavior and that of his young bride. Oh, they both seemed equally infatuated with the other. But my cousin's wife seemed much more comfortable in her new role as wife. It seemed for her a natural fit. Her every movement, her every utterance was graceful, fluid.

My cousin, by contrast, looked like one of those chimpanzees dressed in clothing and trained to play the part of a human, perhaps dressed in the garb of a postal worker and strolling the street delivering mail. There's a hint of reality in the whole scene, but you sense immediately that something isn't quite right. The monkey's movements are exaggerated to the point of awkwardness, and though the beast is doing his best, you can't help but think to yourself, "Hey, that's a monkey dressed like a postal worker."

I had the same reaction to my cousin: "Hey, that's a guy acting like a husband." His every action, his every word seemed grossly overdetermined. Like the monkey, he seemed to be playing a part that was, for him, far from the natural order of things. He was in uncharted territory and doing what he thought husbands should do.

Naturally, he doted on his bride. He lavished her with repeated and outlandish compliments. He wasn't content to refer to his wife merely by her name; rather, she was "my darling wife" or "my gorgeous wife," and when he felt like laying on a stomach-churning sign of affection, she became "my darling, gorgeous wife." Not that husbands shouldn't pile on the praise, but every compliment, every adoring action was offered up in such an exaggerated fashion that even his most sincere efforts made onlookers uncomfortable. At one point, I turned away, dry heaving uncontrollably.

He seemed driven by a compulsion to demonstrate to the world, to his new bride, and even to himself that he was totally in love, that he was the doting and devoted husband. Certainly, he knew what husbands were supposed to do, but he lacked the subtlety of a seasoned veteran who can convey to his wife his undying love in a single look or seemingly inconsequential act.

Take my father-in-law, for example. He's a master of such forms of subtlety. Whenever he attends a potluck dinner with his wife, he is always sure to eat some of her potato salad. Not that he necessarily loves potato salad. He knows that her greatest anxiety at such an event is that no one will eat her potato salad, that when the party's over, her contribution will be the only untouched item on the table. Thus, she sees his gesture as one of many indicators of his regard for her.

He once even planted a willow tree that still grows in their backyard, knowing full well that the willow is a noxious tree, dropping leaves and limbs, and having a root system that can ravage a backyard, underground pipes, and even the foundation of a home. Why did he do it? Because his wife loves willow trees. The tree now stands as an impressive monument of his love for her. Every fall as he rakes the millions of fallen leaves, inwardly praying that the roots haven't infiltrated his home and cursing a tree he sees as a monstrosity of inconvenience, he sings praises to the woman he loves.

Over time I've come to realize that what separates my cousin and my father-in-law is merely experience. Most married men, especially myself, were, in the early days of marriage, like monkeys dressed as postal workers. We were determined to be good husbands and we tried hard—too hard. We were, to say the least, clumsy, even awkward in our attempts to play the part of the good husband. What I've since learned is that this isn't a role we *jump* into. It's a role we *grow* into.

The irony is that marriage throws us into the role woefully unprepared. If we're lucky, we marry patient, understanding women who see through our clumsiness our sincerity and the goodness of our intentions. We hope that they realize that good husbands aren't born, they're made, and developing the habits of a seasoned husband takes time and effort. Opening a door for your wife, greeting her with a kiss, and making sure the last words she hears before going to bed are "I love you," even when you're on a business trip in China, are subtle forms of expression she'll appreciate.

And the point is that husbands do these types of things on a regular basis so they become natural. While the monkey may never fully master the mannerisms of an experienced postal worker, new husbands, I'm convinced, can master the mannerisms of the seasoned husband. Even my father-in-law was, according to my mother-in-law, once as clumsy as a chimpanzee clad in postal garb. So there's hope for my cousin and me and all men if we keep trying.

three

A Climber's Guide to Mount Love-a-Lot:

A Chick-Flick Extravaganza

Sometimes I'm convinced that the gods are toying with us men and that marriage is their favorite playground. Take, for example, one of the saddest realities of married life—how quickly our wives' motors cool off after the honeymoon.

Oh, sure, our married friends warned us as we stood on the threshold of matrimony. They explained, often with frustration in their voices, how they had to devise elaborate schemes to revive their wives' marital appetites. But we were sure that our wives-to-be would live headache-free lives and would be as eager as we are to regularly indulge in the pleasures of married life. After all, their motors seemed to run as steady and hot as ours during courtship. For those of us who were determined to delay these pleasures until marriage, the combined energy generated by mere hand holding was more than enough to power a locomotive.

When the dam finally did give way, we were carried away by a current so strong that resisting was futile. We were engulfed in a flood of emotions so exquisite that we were sure we had crested the pinnacle of our existence, and the real beauty of the experience was that the feelings were mutual. Our wives were swept away in the same fantastic delirium.

Not long after marriage, however, something tragic occurs. While we men are still eager to rise to those majestic heights, preferably on a nightly basis, our wives inexplicably settle comfortably to the flatlands below, and we soon learn that we might sooner drag the most stubborn of mules up the mountain than talk our wives into making the climb with us.

Reluctantly, we accept the fact that we won't be scaling Mount Love-a-Lot with the regularity we'd hoped. And once we've come to appreciate even a weekly ascent, there comes another fatal blow—children.

After the mandatory six-week sojourn through a desert more barren and dry than the one we wandered during early adolescence, we are mystified by our wives' ability to seemingly go indefinite periods of time without the slightest indication of a fleshly appetite. It's not that the motor won't start; rather, it seems she's lost the motor completely.

As we watch our children monopolize our wives' time and energy, we feel a mixture of bitterness and envy. Oh sure, we love our children. We just wish our wives could devote as much attention to us as they do to them. We even recognize that motherhood is draining, and we can't help but understand why she's not interested in mountain climbing at the end of the day.

Nonetheless, there isn't anything we won't try to kick start the motor. To help alleviate her stress, we'll attend to our children with a determination that makes June Cleaver look like a negligent mother. We'll even clean the house with the ferocity of a domestic demon. We reason that if we relieve some of the burden of motherhood, our wives will suddenly find the energy and desire to blast us into oblivion.

And then begins the search for an aphrodisiac, something that will flip the switch and unclog the wheels. If we're lucky enough to stumble onto something that works, we praise the gods that have orchestrated our demise.

Of course, the real tragedy of the situation is that we don't care what it takes to resurrect those premarital appetites, even if it means sacrificing our dignity and self-respect.

I've learned to accept, for example, that other men seem to hold the keys to my wife's motor. Fortunately, these other men tend to be movie stars—men like Brad Pitt and Ewan McGregor. While it's unlikely that my wife will ever leave me for them, I still feel a little insecure.

Sadly (and here comes the pathetic part), I can live with my insecurity. I can even live with the fact that these other men can get my wife to the starting line. In some ways, I feel an indebtedness to them since I'm the one who sees her through to the finish. My gratitude, in fact, has blinded me to just how pathetic I've become. It was only recently that I made this discovery.

My wife and I were watching an adolescent chick flick, one targeting teenage girls and that followed a predictable but effective formula—bad boy meets good girl, good girl redeems bad boy, and the two fall in love. I'm not sure how we ended up renting it, but I'm not sorry we did.

Not long into the movie, my wife developed an infatuation with the teen heartthrob who played the lead role. We were initially on separate couches, but before long, my wife was snuggled up next to me and then on top of me. I was thinking I would need climbing gear before the night was over.

This teenage actor had done in a moment what I often spend months trying to achieve. Was I jealous? Heavens no. If things went well, I planned on sending a thank-you card.

It was at that moment that I realized I had lost all self-respect. I wanted to climb Mount Love-a-Lot so badly that I didn't care what got us to base camp. I just wanted a chance at the peak, and if it took some eighteen-year-old actor to get us going up the path, who cared?

Unfortunately, the movie ended on a tragic note, and as quickly as my wife found the mood I had been searching for, she lost it. It vanished into the recesses of an abyss beyond the scope of human perception, and I was left staring at the top of a mountain I so dearly wanted to climb.

But I learned a valuable lesson. Movies were a means of inspiring my wife. I would just need to be careful and choose films with happy endings. And I would have to act quickly since the mood is fleeting.

I suspect that other women respond in a similar fashion, and we men really shouldn't be surprised. I'm sure we've all been mesmerized by some starlet on the big screen. The difference for us is that we better not let on to our wives that the starlet is what got our engines running. Our wives aren't so desperate that they'll drive a car started by another woman.

One activity that may provide a mutual payoff involves surprising your wife with a proven chick flick. She'll likely appreciate that you picked a movie with her in mind (no need to tell her your real motive). Pop some popcorn and then curl up on the couch together. Do your best to feign a sincere interest in the film and be prepared to head up the path. Oh, and don't forget your climbing gear.

four

The Myth of the Big Spender:
A Homegrown Bouquet of Flowers

I'm convinced that there are two types of men in this world: those who pretend to be big spenders and those who shamelessly let each dollar go with a stubborn reluctance.

Most men fall into the first category, particularly during courtship. On one hand, we accuse the fair sex of shallowness and frivolity when impressing them requires spending more than a few bucks. On the other hand, we admit to our own shallowness in our willingness to become someone we're not, namely the big spender. Indeed, what could be more shallow than using cash to win the love and affection of a woman? Rather than rely on charm, personality, and rugged good looks—a novel proposition, I realize—we drive sports cars, devise the most elaborate and expensive dates imaginable (see the next chapter), and send roses in bulk, all in an effort to woo women. We willingly, even eagerly, live a lie just for the sake of gaining the attention of the opposite sex.

I remember shopping with my wife once during the early stages of our relationship. She was looking for a new outfit and was having trouble deciding between two she liked. Even though I was flat busted and wasn't sure where my next tank of gas would come from, I immediately whipped out the credit card. "Why not buy them both?" I suggested.

In an instant, I was elevated from the status of mere boyfriend to that of superhero. I'd become Credit Card Man, able to hurdle high prices in a single bound, more powerful than an empty wallet, and capable of incurring debt faster than the U.S. government. Throwing her arms around my neck, she exclaimed to me, to the world, "You're the best!" That single act secured a place in her heart forever, and although my act of spontaneous and excessive spending meant riding the bus for a few weeks, it was worth it. She was worth it.

What my wife would tragically learn, however, is that my spontaneous and excessive spending was a hoax, a ploy concocted to convince her that I wasn't just any ordinary guy. The sad truth is, most of us are ordinary, and nothing proves this more than our transformation from big spender to no spender in the wake of our marriage vows.

I remember seeing my wife's credit card receipt after her first trip to the beauty salon just weeks after we were married. "Holy haircut!" I gasped and immediately suggested that she start cutting her own hair. The money she spent on hair-care products alone would have fed us for a month. Friday nights out turned into Friday nights in. "Why go to a movie when we can see it on DVD in a few months?" I reasoned. And vacations turned into weekend jaunts to see the folks—free room and board.

Within months, I'd gone from Credit Card Man to Ultra Cheap, Credit Card Man's arch nemesis.

Now, the shamelessly frugal man is more honest with himself and the woman he loves. He admits and makes no apologies for being, as he likes to put it, thrifty. Such men are, of course, few and far between, and how they ultimately win the love of a woman remains a mystery to me.

From day one of their relationships, they make no pretensions about not wanting to part with their hard-earned money. They shamelessly, and in full view of their dates, present two-for-one coupons when buying movie tickets. They purchase dinner for one at the local buffet and then produce a second fork when the waitress wanders out of view. And despite such behavior—perhaps because of such behavior—they find women willing to accept their marriage proposals.

Who knows? Maybe there are a handful of women out there who are impressed by a man's disciplined spending habits. Or maybe the charm, personality, and rugged good looks of such men are enough to win the heart of a woman. In any case, it's from such a man that I take the following idea.

I have a neighbor who would rather wade hip deep through raw sewage to fix a clogged toilet than pay a plumber to fix it for him. And when it comes to wooing his wife, he insists on the most affordable—that is to say cheap—ways possible. Rather than drop thirty to fifty dollars on roses, he invests a few bucks in seeds, grows his own flowers, and cuts and arranges his own bouquets. I suspect he even uses an old mason jar for a vase. What's most shocking about his cheap alternative to the high cost of flowers is that his wife loves being presented with a homegrown, albeit awkwardly arranged, bouquet.

As I've reflected on my neighbor's frugal approach to flowers, I've come to realize that what his wife appreciates isn't so much the flowers as the care and effort planting and arranging flowers requires. While his garden doesn't cost him much in terms of dollars, it requires time and energy, something we men are at times more reluctant to part with than money. After all, merely having a dozen roses delivered to your wife is certainly easier than mastering the horticulture arts. Could it be that that is what women really want instead of flashy, expensive gifts? Do they want to see in the gifts we bestow on them signs of sacrifice? Based on my neighbor's experience, I would have to say the answer is yes.

So I suggest planting a small garden and cutting and arranging your own bouquets to present to your wife. You might even invest in a nice vase, though there is a certain charm in a mason jar.

It's important, however, that you cut flowers from *your* garden since your wife would probably get a bit upset if you started cutting flowers from hers.

five

The "Truth" in Advertising:

Dinner and a Movie with a Twist

Like most men, I was determined to impress my wife while we were dating. When planning dates, I racked my brain to come up with extraordinary and elaborate dates, dates that would demonstrate to her that she wasn't dating any ordinary guy. I once surprised her with tickets to the ballet and then a late dinner at a five-star restaurant. Surely, I thought, she'll be wooed by my cultured and refined tastes. Unfortunately, I dropped the ball when, at intermission, I assumed the ballet was over. "Wasn't that magnificent? Should we be off to dinner?"

Looking back, I've come to realize that dating is really an elaborate form of deception. Men in particular transform themselves into supermen, of sorts (see the previous chapter). When trying to win the women we love and make them happy, we instantly become more sensitive, more generous, less self-centered, and more willing to do things we detest.

Perhaps deception isn't the right word. Perhaps what dating really is, is a ritual designed to reform and improve our beastly tendencies. When not dating, we tend to move about in packs of other men and degenerate into creatures not fit for female society. Consider that only men admire and find humorous our ability to discharge intestinal gasses on command.

Dating, then, is really a way of reclaiming our better selves, a way of warding off that demon known as macho masculinity. And if we stop dating after marriage, we run the risk of degenerating into a creature even more hideous, more repulsive than the single, unattached man: we become hideous, repulsive married men. We might even get to a point where we shamelessly and with a perverse pride expel intestinal gasses within earshot of our wives.

Perhaps more tragically, we assume that marriage signals an end to dating and the need to put our best selves forward. Saying "I do," I thought, meant I'd no longer have to feign an interest in the ballet or submit myself to the excruciating anguish of date planning. I had won my wife through courtship, and my reward was a license to be myself, right?

Undoubtedly, marriage is proof that we did something right during courtship. All our ploys while dating worked; against all odds, our wives fell in love with us. But have we forgotten what worked? Or have we just stopped doing what worked? If so, chances are our wives have forgotten why they fell in love with us. Consequently, we probably need to jog our own memories and theirs from time to time. This means that dinner and a movie probably aren't enough. Yes, we've got to keep planning elaborate and creative dates even after marriage.

To help jog her memory, I suggest making the ordinary

slightly extraordinary—what I like to refer to as dinner and a movie with a twist.

Here's the thing. My wife and I actually enjoy dinner and a movie, perhaps the most ordinary and traditional of courtship rituals in our culture. While dating, however, this was a bit too humdrum to impress; after marriage, dinner and a movie can become equally humdrum.

One way to spice up dinner and a movie is to surprise your wife at the end of the evening with a little moonlight dessert. Before the date, prepare some fruit—grapes, chocolate-dipped strawberries—perhaps some cheese and crackers, sparkling cider, or whatever beverage you and your wife enjoy drinking, and put it all into a cooler or basket in the trunk of your car. Include a blanket and perhaps a romantic CD, and you've got the makings of a romantic climax to an otherwise ordinary evening. When choosing a location, I recommend somewhere quiet and dark, such as a park, a scenic overlook, or the fifty-yard line of your old high school football field.

All of this should be a surprise. On the drive home, take a detour, pull into the park, and pop the trunk. If you really want to impress, include nice china, crystal goblets, and some roses. If the sprinklers don't get you, your wife will certainly be impressed with your creative date planning, and she'll perhaps recall why she fell in love with you in the first place.

six

"There's No 'I' in 'Us,' . . . or Is There?":

Draw Her a Bath

One of the remarkable features of dating is how it brings two individuals, perhaps even fiercely independent individuals, to a state of utter inseparability. During the initial stages of falling in love, couples go to completely irrational, even ridiculous, lengths to see each other, if only for a few minutes.

I once drove thirty miles in a blinding snowstorm to see my wife for a mere fifteen minutes while she was between jobs. We spent every spare moment with each other, and when we weren't together, we kept close tabs on the other's activities. My mental and emotional health depended on the knowledge of where she was every moment of every day.

And then came a fateful Saturday in April when she slipped outside my radar. She wasn't at work. She wasn't at home. Her friends hadn't seen her in days and hardly had seen her at all since she'd been dating me. Where could she be?

I considered calling the local hospitals and even the police. Surely, something awful must have happened—a car accident or a fatal slash to her leg while shaving. Or worse yet, perhaps she was with somebody else. The mere thought turned my innards to Jell-O and me into a shivering, cold blob of insecure masculinity. This was serious.

Then, unexpectedly and without warning, she turned up. As quickly and imperceptibly as she'd gone, she materialized out of thin air with a Dr. Pepper in hand. I took her in my arms, thanked God she was alive, and then asked, "Where in the Hades have you been?" A bit startled, she replied, "At the home and garden show."

"Home and garden show? With whom?"

"No one," she answered. "By myself."

I immediately recognized that this was a critical moment in our relationship. Do I reveal my insecurities by pushing her on the point? Did I trust her enough to believe she was actually alone? I chose, instead, a less direct route. "Why didn't you call me? I love home and garden shows."

Then came a response as painful as if she had been with another guy: "I just needed some time to myself." *Time to myself,* I thought, *There's no "I" in "us."* What had I done that necessitated this sudden withdrawal? I responded with a profound, "Oh," and not wanting to show my discontent, redirected the conversation to the home and garden show.

While she enthusiastically described all the decorating ideas she had gathered, I noticed her energetic smile. She seemed pleased, happy. Such an effect from a few hours alone? Even time with me didn't always produce these kinds of results. If only she had been with someone else. The pain certainly could not have been more acute. Why would she want to be alone, without me, even for a few hours? Had I become, in a few short months, repulsive?

Then, amidst my crushing anxieties, something remarkable happened, something truly magnificent. As her attention turned from her decorating ideas, she became fixated on me, the pitiable imbecile who was, at that moment, tormented by an irrational and pathetic insecurity. She seemed more committed to me and our relationship.

Time to herself turned out to be a good thing, and experience has confirmed this revelation. Both my wife and I return from such moments more focused on the other and less irritated with each other's shortcomings, and we revel more in our shared company.

If I'm right on this point, husbands would do well to create some time for their wives to be alone. This is especially true for women with children. While you can always send them to a home and garden show, sometimes they need the calm of an empty house. So draw a hot bath, light some scented candles, and take the kids to McDonald's. You might even buy your wife a magazine or two, a bottle of her favorite beverage, and some fruit to snack on in the tub. Let her know that you and the kids will be gone for several hours. She can enjoy her bath and do whatever she wants.

Although you'll likely return from McDonald's frazzled, perhaps even ready to step in front of a speeding car, you can bet that your wife will be more relaxed and more in love with you—a combination that will surely cure the mania of McDonald's playland.

seven

For Love of the Game:

Throw Her a Party

I read once that one of the fundamental differences between men and women is that men tend to be competitive and combative in their relationships with others, whereas women are more inclined to be cooperative and nurturing. While the first half of this hypothesis seems perfectly plausible, I can't help but take issue with the second.

Whether driven by genetics or culture, we men certainly thrive on competition. Nothing does our hearts as much good as triumphing over friend and foe alike. We thrive on the defeat and anguish of any and all opponents, no matter the contest.

And one of the more remarkable features of the masculine psyche is how we can turn even the most trivial activity into a highly competitive game. In fact, I'm not sure we're capable of functioning at all unless an activity includes teams, an objective, winners, and losers. Take, for example, the following scenario.

Two male friends are sitting at a bus stop. One friend picks up a small stone and throws it at a nearby street sign, missing by the slimmest of margins. The other friend lets go with a laugh and a snide remark regarding his friend's feeble attempt to hit the sign. The second friend then picks up a stone and hurls it with all the precision he can muster, hitting the sign dead on.

Not to be outdone, the first friend hurls another rock. Before long the two have defined an elaborate set of rules for "Who Can Hit the Street Sign," a game unlikely to find its way into the annals of the great gaming traditions of Western culture but one in which the level of intensity and desire to best one's opponent rivals the Super Bowl.

And the stakes are nearly as high. After losing the first game, the loser, unwilling to accept defeat, suggests that they play again, only this time the loser must go to a nearby street corner, drop his pants to his knees, and yell at the top of his lungs, "I'm the biggest loser in the world!"

Men take pride in the slightest of victories, whether it be the loudest burp, the longest sustained expulsion of intestinal gas, or the most ribs consumed during a single sitting at the local Barbecue Beef Pit Extravaganza.

But the beauty of such seemingly trivial contests—yes, *beauty* is the right word—is how competition among men paradoxically builds friendships and can bring even the fiercest of enemies together. When all the blood, sweat, and tears have been shed, men develop a mutual respect for each other and come to appreciate their rival's intense desire to win at all costs. Even after bloodying their knuckles in mortal combat, antagonists can come together to share a glass.

Once in sixth grade I engaged a hated rival in a brawl to determine who was the toughest hombre on the playground. A broken wrist (mine) and a split lip (his) later, the two of us wiped our wounds, shook hands, and supped from the communal waters of the nearest fountain. In minutes, the two of us had beat the other senseless and become the best of friends.

Women, on the other hand, hate with an intensity that is only aggravated by engagement with the enemy, but there is a kind of beauty in their engagement as well. While men generally make no effort to mask their animosity for their male rivals, women show their worst enemies the greatest kindness. This, I suppose, accounts for the view that women are supposedly less competitive than men.

But don't be mistaken.

The exaggerated smiles, the excessive compliments, and all the pleasantries that give the impression that two women are the best of friends have the same effect as an obscene joke about one's mother or a right hook.

I remember being with a girl I once dated and running into an old high school classmate of hers. The two hugged, exchanged the phrase "It's so good to see you" a dozen or so times, and even suggested that they meet for lunch one day soon. After parting, my date dug her fingernails into my arm and said, "I hate her."

Have I missed something? I wondered.

"Have you ever seen anyone so fake in your life?" she went on.

No comment.

"So you're not going to call her for lunch?" I asked.

"Not in this life," came the response.

It turned out that every smile and every compliment regarding how the other looked was, in some perplexing way, a calculated insult. My date had mentioned two or three times how her high school chum hadn't changed a bit, when, in reality, she had gained more than fifty pounds. My date still wore the same dress size she had in high school, a tremendous source of pride for her and angst for her "friend." Clearly, this triumph brought my date a great deal of satisfaction, like winning the Super Bowl.

Perhaps nothing demonstrates the competitiveness of women more than the pleasure they derive from being adored by a man in public, especially in front of other women. What man doesn't dread the phrase, "Why can't you be more like so-and-so's husband?"

This phrase indicates two things: one, you're failing miserably as a husband; and two, another woman has bested your wife in "Who's Got the Best Man," a game even more intense than "Who Can Hit the Street Sign."

In suggesting that women thrive on public displays of male devotion, my intention is not to trivialize love. Certainly, women want to be loved for love's sake. Letting the world and other women see just how much they are loved is merely a bonus.

For this reason, I suggest you throw your wife a party. You can throw her a surprise birthday party or a party to celebrate an achievement or a party just to celebrate her. The party can be elaborate, requiring extensive planning or a simple event to which you invite a few friends.

So long as the party is for your wife and provides you an opportunity to show the world—perhaps even a few of her mortal enemies—that she's the master of your universe, you'll likely avoid the phrase, "Why can't you be more like so-and-so's husband." More important, you will give your wife the satisfaction of knowing that every man who attended her party will be hearing that same phrase from their wives on the drive home.

eight

Living in Eden:
The Marriage Contract

I imagine the first time a husband realized that the honeymoon was over was shortly after Adam and Eve were expelled from the Garden of Eden.

Reflecting on the ease of his existence while in the garden, I can see Adam confronting Eve.

"Now, why'd you have to go and eat the forbidden fruit?"

And before Adam can say another word, the once affable Eve immediately turns on the unsuspecting Adam and lets loose with a flurry of words never before heard in the history of the world.

"You mean to tell me that this is my fault? If you hadn't left me alone to be tempted by that talking serpent, none of this would have happened. And besides, if you were so concerned about the fruit, why didn't you cut down the darn tree in the first place?"

By the time Eve ends her tirade, Adam, completely convinced that he alone is at fault for their fall from grace, cowers in shame, makes a thousand apologies, and accepts total and full responsibility.

Adam learns in a moment what every husband has since learned by the same hard experience: it's our fault.

And generally it is. On those occasions when we cling to the idea that we aren't entirely at fault, our wives will convince us that we are. It's probably best to accept the inevitable rather than resist (see chapter 27).

Imagine Adam weeks later, banished from the garden into the harsh reality of the real world, tilling the ground and eating his bread by the sweat of his brow. Looking at Eve, his once-perfect wife, he notices that she's put on a few pounds. The brightness of her eyes has dimmed; she looks tired all the time. And he sees in her face a wrinkle here and there. All because this woman lacked a little restraint!

Before long, he hardly recognizes Eve, and he can hardly remember Eden. Those days are distant, the honeymoon long gone.

This is a moment Adam never imagined while in the garden. It's a moment most men can't imagine as they embark on their married lives, but it's a day that can easily come unless we remember what got us to the marriage altar in the first place and recommit ourselves to doing those things that will keep our wives from metamorphosing into unrecognizable creatures.

The irony here is that we may, in fact, be responsible for what our wives become. What if in becoming inattentive, insensitive husbands, we transform our wives into women we no longer recognize?

After all, where exactly was Adam when the serpent

beguiled Eve? He certainly wasn't with her. Perhaps she felt isolated, alone; the serpent and the fruit may have filled a void created by a negligent husband.

And to think that Eve has been vilified for centuries for the Fall. Perhaps it *was* Adam's fault.

The point is, we wield more control over the fate of our married lives than we realize, and one way to remind and recommit ourselves to the kind of behavior that will help us remain in Eden is to produce what I call a marriage contract.

Like any legal contract, the marriage contract should be written in formal, matter-of-fact language, and it is, above all else, binding. Your contract might begin like this: "I, Brett C. McInelly, in an effort to demonstrate my love for my wife, Kristin M. McInelly, hereby commit on this, the first day of June, to do those things that will promote the happiness of the aforementioned Kristin McInelly and build a successful marriage." This might then be followed with a detailed list of things you intend to do to promote your wife's happiness. You might even include some kind of penalty for your failure to come through with your end of the bargain. The contract should be typed and signed. I recommend putting it in a nice frame before presenting it to your wife.

In a way, Adam and Eve were expelled from the garden for a breech of contract. If we live up to our commitments to each other, perhaps our marriages won't stray too far from our own gardens.

nine

"I Have Nothing to Wear":
Surprise Her with a New Outfit

One of the most oft-repeated phrases heard in my home is, "I have nothing to wear." Ironically, my wife makes this statement while standing and staring with a bewildered look at a closet full of clothes, some of them worn only once or twice.

I, on the other hand, have a couple of outfits that I manage to adapt to any event imaginable: two suits and a sports coat for formal occasions, a few pair of khaki pants and a golf shirt for less-formal occasions, and a pair of jeans and a T-shirt or two, sometimes with a pithy, perhaps even slightly off-color remark written across the back for those outings on which class and sophistication aren't prerequisites.

My whole dressing strategy involves rotating the few outfits I own so as not to wear the same thing twice in row. For example, if I wear my olive-colored suit and silk tie to a wedding, I'll chose my blue blazer to the following funeral. Rotating my slightly off-color T-shirts is even more critical since they generally make an impression. Nothing proves more humiliating than to have someone say, "Hey, didn't you wear that T-shirt to the last barbecue?"

While I'm personally impressed with the economy and flexibility of my wardrobe, I find its longevity even more impressive. Some of the formal outfits, only worn a dozen or so times in the past fifteen years, are still in excellent condition. They're even still fashionable in some states.

As I'm deciding between olive green and navy blue, my wife is utterly befuddled, you would think, by the sheer volume of choices before her. Unable to make a decision, she helplessly throws her arms in the air and exclaims, "I have nothing to wear."

I suggest that she wear the tight-fitting, cream-colored dress: "You look stunning in it, darling."

"Are you kidding?" she replies, "I wore that dress twenty-seven months ago to your brother's wedding."

"Yes, but what are the odds that anyone at my work party was at my brother's wedding?" I counter. "And besides, while you do look stunning in that dress, do you really think anyone will remember what you wore twenty-seven months ago?"

Any experienced husband recognizes the futility of such questions. For whatever reason, my wife believes that other people possess for her wardrobe the Rolodex-like memory she has for my marital blunders. Just as she can recall in an instant my insensitivity on a day in 1994, she fervently believes that someone will be able to recall on sight an outfit she wore years before.

I admit that I'm no Ralph Lauren, but I'm perplexed by

my wife's fashion sense. While she undoubtedly would claim that I have no sense at all, and she's probably right, I wonder if there's something more to her lack of clothing options than hypersensitivity to being seen in the same outfit twice. Perhaps at bottom is a compulsive desire to accumulate as many articles of clothing as possible. Like men and power tools, do women achieve a certain degree of satisfaction from merely owning clothes—some that may only be worn a single time?

When we tiled the bathroom, I could have rented a tile saw for a fraction of the cost of buying one. Nonetheless, I chose to buy, knowing that I would rarely, if ever, use the saw after we finished the bathroom. And yet I'm overcome with pride every time I see it sitting in the corner of my garage collecting dust. I sometimes lure unsuspecting male friends there just so they can remark with envy, "Ah, you have a tile saw!"

Is it possible that women, like men, are actually keeping score, tallying up the number of outfits owned and worn by others?

If I'm right about women and their wardrobes, presenting your wife with a new outfit for a particular occasion would certainly be a nice surprise. Such a gift would add to an ever-expanding wardrobe and help propel her well ahead of her female acquaintances.

Imagine calling your wife from work, asking her to dinner at a fine restaurant, and then stopping by a lady's clothing store on your way home to pick out a new outfit. Then, as your wife muses over what to wear, you spring it on her: "Why not wear this?" You might even have the outfit gift wrapped.

Or imagine your wife agonizing for weeks in advance over an upcoming wedding. She drops one hint after another about how she has nothing to wear and how so and so will be at the wedding and so forth. You pretend to ignore her, perhaps suggesting that she just wear such and such dress. Then, a few days before the wedding, you produce a beautiful new dress. Not only have you prevented a potentially traumatic moment for your wife, but you have also ensured that she wears something you like.

Perhaps the only thing more irritating than hearing, "I have nothing to wear" is saying, "You look great" when your wife wears a dress that you inwardly find hideous.

Even more than power tools, we men relish an opportunity to show off our wives, particularly to other men. Consciously or not, we sense that only a small miracle accounts for our wives accepting our marriage proposals. Thus, when our wives look particularly striking, we stand a little taller, as if to insinuate, "I'm with her." Dressed in an outfit you surprised her with, she will be overjoyed to see her wardrobe expanded by one, and you'll be delighted to see her adorned in an outfit of your choosing.

Now the down side. If your taste in women's clothing is at odds with your wife's, or if you have no taste at all, this might prove a difficult and potentially dangerous task. Imagine the predicament you put your wife in if you produce a dress that she finds repulsive. The only thing worse than being caught in the same outfit twice, I suspect, is being caught in an outfit your wife can't stand. So while she appreciates your thoughtfulness, she inwardly resents you for putting her in a position where she must choose between her reputation and your feelings.

For those men who lack confidence or experience choosing women's clothing, I would suggest that you consult your wife's best friend or the sales clerk at the clothing store. Whether working alone or with someone else, you need to choose wisely, and while you want her to wear an outfit you personally find attractive, you might reconsider the tight leather jumper adorned with steel studs and tassels. I learned this one the hard way.

ten

Self-Discipline:
The No-Strings-Attached Full-Body Massage

My wife is convinced that almost anything I do for her is intended as a prelude to conjugal relations. After reading this book, you might think so as well. The sad truth is, she's probably right.

Take cuddling, for example. In theory, my wife, like most women, loves to cuddle. In practice, she knows from experience that I'm incapable of *just* cuddling. When I roll over in bed, nuzzle up to her back, and wrap my arms around her, I immediately feel her whole body go tense. And I . . . well, let's just say I go a little tense myself.

Sadly, my wife knows that I'm not going to let her sleep until I'm not tense anymore. Even when I initiate cuddling with the best of intentions—to appease her needs—I find myself becoming less and less interested in just cuddling. At this point, my wife sees cuddling as an impediment to sleep.

Given my inability to *just* cuddle, my next suggestion might seem like an impossibility, and I admit that a no-strings-attached full-body massage might be beyond the physical limits of most men. However, the key here is her pleasure, not yours. The goal is to help her relax, and I guarantee that she won't be able to relax if she knows at the back of her mind that you're just interested in getting what you want.

The first time I said, "I want to give you a massage," my wife heard, "I want to fool around." And even if my intentions were pure, who was I kidding? Could I possibly *just* give her a massage? Is it any wonder that she repeatedly turned down my offers? And when she finally accepted, it wasn't long before she was saying, "I told you so."

The point I'm trying to make is that this idea requires a certain amount of self-mastery as well as a hard sell. You've got to be able to convince her (as well as yourself) that you're *just* offering her a massage. And if you do sell yourself and your wife on the idea, following through is even more difficult and will require eunuchlike self-discipline.

My advice is to catch her coming out of the shower. You might light a few candles, put on some soft music, and invest in some massage oil, not the flavored kind you get at adult novelty stores but some actual massage oil. Let her get comfortable on the bed, and then go to work. Your wife will likely be as tense as you are for the first several minutes. She'll be thinking, *It won't be long now.*

With any luck, she'll drift off to sleep before she gets a chance to say, "I told you so." And with even more luck, she'll awake the next morning totally shocked and relaxed. She may even recognize that you're still tense and feel compelled to relieve your tenseness.

Of course, I would never be so bold as to recommend a no-strings-attached massage without offering a tip or two on how to develop eunuchlike self-discipline. While I'm hardly a master, I've found that imagining a nudist retirement home often robs me of my thunder.

eleven

If It Doesn't Kill Ya:
Do Something You Don't Like

When my wife and I got married, I acknowledged, with some reluctance, that certain features of my previous life would be forfeited when I uttered, "I do." I realized I wouldn't be able to invest as much time pursuing my passion for fishing and golf as I had while single.

Don't get me wrong. I was perfectly willing to make such sacrifices for the woman I loved. But trading in hip waders for chick flicks wasn't easy, even when done in the name of love, and a part of me felt a deep sense of loss for my past life.

Then, at the moment I was ready to accept the seemingly inevitable, a revelation came in a flash of stupefying light. Why not take her with me? Certainly, once she felt the exhilaration of fighting a three-pound rainbow trout or the euphoria of a well-struck golf shot, she would hound me for opportunities to do both. A giddy smile came to my face as I imagined my wife approaching me on a lazy Saturday morning and suggesting, "Honey, why don't we grab the fishing poles and head up to the lake?"

As I pondered my first move, I knew it would be a hard sell. Never before had she expressed the least degree of interest in fishing or golf, even during those early days of courtship when we both pretended to enjoy things we really hated in order to impress the other. I once suffered for hours through a bridal show, all the while acting as if I'd been planning my own wedding since I was a boy.

I knew I needed to come up with the perfect pitch, and I would have to mask my own self-interest. No, I couldn't ask her to take up fishing and golf for my sake. Besides, she might ask for something in return. She might ask me to take up quilting or arts and crafts!

I decided to convince her that fishing and golf would improve our relationship by bringing us closer together. "Imagine," I explained, "the two of us waist deep in a mountain stream, surrounded by beautiful scenery and listening to a symphony of running water. What could be more romantic?"

To my wife's credit, she gave fishing a shot. She braved the mosquitoes and a wicked sunburn—hardly the romantic experience I promised—for me. Swatting bugs and inwardly longing for a shower, she toughed it out, knowing how much I enjoy fishing.

I eventually came to the conclusion that she would likely never share my passion for fishing or golf. I've learned, however, that she at least has enough passion for me that she'll endure a few mosquitoes while I battle a trout.

I still don't fish or golf nearly as much as I would like.

Perhaps no man does, including those who aren't even married. And if the truth be told, I can't get enough of my wife's company either, so I brave my share of home-decorating shows. I've found that my wife genuinely appreciates my willingness to participate in such activities, especially when I'm a good sport and do the best I can to hide my pain. Of course, she still knows it hurts, but that's how she knows I'm doing it for her.

Perhaps one of the best ways to demonstrate our love is to do something she loves but we hate: a trip to the mall? A chick flick? Ballroom dance lessons? The more the activity makes us shudder in horror, the more our wives will likely acknowledge our willingness to endure it with a smile. If we're really lucky, our wives will thank us for indulging them by suggesting that we go play a round of golf with our friends.

twelve

Feather Dusters and Fishnet Stockings:

Play Maid for a Day

Last October my wife and I took our kids to pick out Halloween costumes. My son, who loves action figures, choose a ninja costume; my daughter, a dress-up fanatic, went with an elaborate princess dress; and my youngest, a timid little girl afraid of her own shadow, was terrified by the ghoulish masks and just wanted to get out of the store as fast as possible. My wife, a lover of holidays in general and especially Halloween, couldn't resist and was soon perusing costumes for herself. She chose a witch's outfit, much to my chagrin.

My children, with the exception of the timid little one, selected costumes that made manifest their own internalized fantasies of themselves, and I must admit that it did my heart good to see their respective choices. What father wouldn't be overjoyed to see his son grow up to be a ninja and his daughter a princess? I chose to dress up like Indiana Jones that Halloween. To live a life of adventure, carry a gun and a whip, and always get the girl—what could be more grand?

Obviously, my wife chose to go another route with her choice. I doubt seriously that she entertains fantasies involving witchcraft. No, she sees Halloween the way many people do— as an opportunity to explore the darker side of her personality.

Nonetheless, I wasn't especially happy with her choice, and I pushed hard for another costume, one of those sexy French maid outfits. She certainly couldn't have missed the dozen or so subtle hints I dropped in the store. "Look, honey, a French maid costume. I'll bet you'd look great in that!" "A witch? Sure, you'd make a great witch, but you'd make an even better French maid." "Did I mention that they have a French maid costume?"

As we paraded the children around the neighborhood that Halloween, I thought longingly on the French maid costume. I admit, my wife made a great witch. Not that the transition from loving wife and mother to scary witch wasn't a leap for her. Even in her worst moods, she's a far cry from the wickedest of witches. She just put a lot into her costume, including the finest details. The wart on her nose almost looked real.

But I wondered why she was so unreceptive to my suggestion. After all, I had gone with the Indiana Jones costume partly at her request. Thankfully, she concealed her disappointment when the costume didn't exactly transform me into Harrison Ford. But the point is, I would have dressed up as the back end of a donkey to see her in the French maid costume.

Imagining the fishnet stockings and the high-cut skirt while staring at the wart on her face was almost more than I could bear. "Why not the French maid costume?"

Since that Halloween, I've become less obsessed with why my wife chose to ignore my hints regarding the French maid costume and more interested in my fixation with it. On one hand, my obsession with the costume is obvious. It can be traced to the same part of my psyche that feels cheated if my wife and I leave the mall without visiting the Victoria's Secret store.

On the other hand, there seems to be something more to my obsession. After all, if I want my wife to wear something sleek and sexy, I generally just need to ask. She has a wardrobe full of lingerie.

No, the French maid costume offered something that lingerie doesn't—the idea of a scantily clad woman whose sole purpose in life is to serve me. The costume would have provided, if only for a night, an opportunity to imagine myself as master of the house. This fantasy, more so than the fishnet stockings, accounts for my disappointment that Halloween.

Imagining my wife dressed like a French maid and clutching a feather duster even changed my whole attitude toward housework; it suddenly became sexy. Gone was the image of my wife with disheveled hair and grubby clothes. Instead, all I could see was oo-la-la.

Curiously, my wife has always found housework sexy, at least when I'm the one doing it. And I don't even need to be wearing my steel-studded leather briefs. The image of me hunkered over the toilette with scrubber in hand charges my wife in ways that even a heavy metal love ballad can't. She goes weak in the knees every time she sees me clutching a bottle of 409 or unloading the dishwasher. And if I really want to rock her world, I take it to the next level: I move from surface to deep cleaning.

What is deep cleaning? It essentially involves cleaning in places most men would never imagine need cleaning, places that are not within our immediate view. You'd be amazed at the mess that collects behind the fridge. Lint, year-old meatballs, and spilled milk. Amazingly, milk hardens into a solid over time!

Voluntarily clean an area like this and brace yourself for an eruption of feminine passion. Your wife might even corner you in the kitchen. And if you really want to impress, set aside an entire Saturday, or take a day off from work to scour and scrub, wash and wax, and spit and shine. After the wife recovers from her initial shock, she'll be overcome by how unbelievably sexy you are while pushing a vacuum.

thirteen

Suicide by Sentiment:
Make Her a Greeting Card

Nothing is more excruciating than trolling the rows and rows of greeting cards in the local grocery store. Two things in particular make this experience especially painful: first, the sheer volume of cards to choose from; and second, the horribly pathetic inscriptions on most cards. Perusing one card after another is like being drowned in a raging river of sentimental drivel.

What's worse is that I willfully take the plunge—suicide by sentiment. In my futile search for just the right card, I wade through card after card, reading one limp inscription after another, all the while hoping to find the one that will express my own sappy thoughts. By the time I'm through, I want to retreat into a world without emotion or feeling, a world numb to the beatings of the human heart.

In such moments, I wonder if I'm not an unfeeling ogre. After all, I've seen people reduced to tears by the same greeting card that made me want to throw up. I've stood next to these people in the grocery store. As I've watched them devolve into a blubbering heap of flesh, I've wondered what's wrong with me—am I so jaded and heartless that I've lost my capacity to feel?

I then realize that my problem isn't a lack of an emotional response; my problem is that I expected to find poetry in the greeting card section of the grocery store. I mean, who in the world writes these cards anyway? Does anyone know? I suspect most are failed poets and novelists.

Moreover, isn't it a bit presumptuous on the part of greeting card companies to assume that they have a card for every occasion and every feeling of love, gratitude, grief, and emotion experienced by our species? Certainly, the sheer volume of cards to choose from attests to their efforts, and while we might grant these companies a little leeway for seemingly good intentions, the price of the average greeting card immediately recasts the entire industry in a less-redeeming light.

The creators of greeting cards have the audacity to package pathetic expressions of the heart and carry them to market for a ridiculous price. Oh, sure, Shakespeare himself was out to make a buck, but at least his efforts were worthy of the shilling it cost to attend *Romeo and Juliet*.

My remedy to the greeting card dilemma is simple: create your own greeting cards. Of course, there are no guarantees that you'll produce anything but pathetic drivel yourself, but at least it will be your drivel and will come closer to expressing what's in your heart than the ramblings of some unknown would-be poet. What's more, your wife will be overcome, not so much by your words but by your effort.

I recommend going to a local craft store (don't be surprised if you're the only man there) and buy some high-grade construction paper, some cute little stamps and paper punches, some ribbon, and paints or colored markers. You might even be able to find a card-making kit. Yes, they do make them. Then, find a place where you are least likely to be seen, particularly by other men, and go to work. Even if you're artistically impaired and produce a card that looks like the one you made your mother in kindergarten, you're wife will love it, and here's how I know.

I'm going to make an admission that may shock my male readers. I can make such an admission only because I'm so utterly secure in my own manhood. Recently, at a family reunion, I found myself watching a group of female relatives sitting around a table making greeting cards. One of them had brought an elaborate greeting card kit and the rest flocked to the table, which instantly became a center of industry and chatter.

As boredom and curiosity overcame me, I sat in the midst of the industry and chatter, took a piece of construction paper in one hand, a pair of scissors in the other, and began the process of designing and crafting my own card. The women were speechless and amazed; the men horrified and disgusted. My wife—really the only one whose opinion really matters—was surprised but impressed. Crafty herself, she had no idea I had any artistic inclinations.

And here comes the most startling admission of all: I enjoyed it. Again, only a man like myself, one so assured of his masculinity, could come clean the way I have here.

When I was through, I had produced a card that rivals any you'll find in the grocery store. This isn't to say that my card doesn't ooze with the sappy ramblings of a would-be poet; it does. But they're *my* sappy ramblings, and they say exactly what I want to say. And my wife loves it, not for its artistic merit but because I made it myself.

fourteen

Girls and Their Dads:

Read Her a Bedtime Story

No matter how long two people date before getting married, the phrase "I do" opens a book on one's spouse previously unread, perhaps not even seen sitting on the shelf during courtship.

Like most husbands, I thought I knew my wife exceptionally well—well enough to take the monumental step of matrimony. A few months into our marriage, however, I discovered a feature of her personality that was beyond my wildest imaginings. The first time this feature reared its ugly head, I was dumbfounded.

Looking for a little intellectual stimulation, I initiated a debate with her, purposefully taking a stance to which I knew she would be vehemently opposed. I enjoy a little verbal wrangling from time to time. Perhaps this side of my personality took her by surprise.

In any case, I soon learned that my wife detests conflict, which is to say, she didn't approve of my holding an opinion she didn't share. Proceeding in what I thought was a cool and collected manner, I watched her become more and more irritated. "How can you think that way?" she snapped. As I pushed the argument further, she turned red, her words stammered to a halt, and without warning, she hurled the TV remote across the room and smacked me in the head.

Argument over.

I'm not sure what was more profound—the pain or my disbelief that the woman I loved had just hit me with the remote. What was even more disturbing is that she was frantically looking for other lose objects to hurl as projectiles.

In that moment I realized for the first time that there was a side to my wife's personality I'd never seen before. My wife, as loving and sweet a woman as she is, had a disposition toward violence!

I couldn't help but think that her action constituted spousal abuse in some states. I imagined myself running from safe house to safe house, trying to avoid the next well-aimed remote. At the very least, I figured I'd better start budgeting for electronics repairs.

Fortunately, time has demonstrated that my wife's inclination to hurl household objects manifests itself only on rare occasions, and at the risk of sounding like the self-effacing victim, I generally deserve a good shot to the head once and while.

And my realization of the strength and precision of my wife's throwing arm hardly compares with the startling realization my wife made in that same moment—that she hadn't married her father.

I don't mean to imply here that my wife fits Freud's paradigm for parent-child relations. Her admiration for her father is not nearly that warped. If she suffers from any ailment relating to her father, that ailment would be hero worship. In my wife's eyes, her father represents the pinnacle of manhood, husbandhood, and fatherhood. He is the standard by which I am measured in her eyes. If her religion didn't prohibit idol worship, I'm not sure she wouldn't erect some kind of graven image in his honor.

And what is more remarkable than the profundity of her admiration for her father is her belief that, upon marriage, I would magically metamorphose into his exact copy. She assumed the words "I do" would suddenly cause all the flaws and imperfections I manifested while dating to disappear. I would emerge from the marriage sanctum a new man, born again to a life of intense devotion and sensitivity. Most important, I would never contradict or disagree with her.

After hurling the remote, my wife uttered the fatal words that shattered the glass house that had become her world: "My dad would never do that!"

My first impulse was to say, "Well, you aren't married to your father." But in those words I realized that that was exactly the point. Of course she wasn't married to her father, but my insensitivity had poignantly proven that her husband wasn't anything like her father, and that was a frightening realization for both of us.

While I don't worship my father-in-law in the same way my wife does, I certainly admire him. I want to treat my wife with the same kind of respect and courtesy he treats my mother-in-law. When I don't I feel like a failure.

Of course, I'll never be my father-in-law. Even my wife has learned to accept this fact. The best I can do is try to emulate those qualities I most admire. And I can father my wife occasionally, perhaps by tucking her into bed and reading her a bedtime story. Most men, including myself, enjoy being mothered a bit. It thus stands to reason that women appreciate being fathered from time to time.

Of course, married women probably would prefer a romance novel to *Goldilocks and the Three Bears*. For those women with more sophisticated tastes, you might choose a classic like *Wuthering Heights* or a Jane Austen novel. You might even read a Shakespeare play together. Or you might read her a self-help book for couples, a book designed to strengthen and improve the quality of marital relationships like the one you're reading. The point is to choose something she enjoys and read it to her or read it together. Read it in bed or snuggled on the sofa in front of the fireplace. Chances are, the reading will lead to talking, and the talking will lead to discovery. You might even discover a side of your wife you've never seen before.

fifteen

The Thrill of Victory, The Agony of Defeat:

Skip the Big Game for a Night Out with Your Wife

My seeming lack of emotion in matters of the heart is a source of great angst for my wife. Tears, she believes, are a sure sign of true love. Unfortunately, I can't muster a single drop when professing my undying devotion. To make matters worse, most sporting events and some movies cause me to sob like a woman in the throws of postpartum depression. And if I watch a movie about sports, I metamorphose into a blubbering train wreck. I'm still not sure I've fully recovered from *Rudy*.

Yet my proclamations of love are generally delivered in

emotion-free and tearless expressions. I try to explain that tears are no proof of a man's love. I even once told my wife that those men who say "I love you" between sobs are actually faking it—not necessarily their love but their tears.

And if being moved to tears by a bunch of grown men piling on top of each other after winning the World Series isn't pathetic enough, my emotional investment in the experience of watching even a regular season game is admittedly disturbing.

I never realized just how pathetic I was until I watched a game for the first time with my wife. From the opening kick off, I launched into an animated discussion with the television. I naturally scolded the referees for every bad call. I insisted, with a few expletives, that a player be benched for a bonehead mistake. When the other team scored the go-ahead touchdown, I rose from the couch, hurled a pillow across the room, and collapsed to the floor. When my team took back the lead, I danced around the couch and did a little jig, all the while taunting the other team: "You stink, you stink, you stink!"

And then I realized that my wife hadn't joined in. She sat staring, horrified by the spectacle in front of her. Her face asked a sobering question: "Who is this raging lunatic I've married?" For a moment, I saw myself through her eyes and I too shuddered in disbelief. I had stepped off the edge into my own heart of darkness—"the horror, the horror."

But I quickly snapped back out of my senses to realize that my team had won! Who cared what my wife thought? Who cared if I was on the verge of delirium? My team had won! This single fact would sustain me for the week to come, until the next game.

But what if my team had lost? My emotional state would be affected for days, even weeks, and the bigger the game, the harder the fall. Friends and family might even order a suicide watch.

My wife still looks on with horror every time I watch a game, but she seems to have accepted the fact that every weekend I give myself—body, heart, and soul—to the next first down, a game-winning homerun, or the agony of defeat. And yet I can't muster a single tear when saying, "I love you."

I'm convinced that most men invest as much emotion into sporting events as I do. I'm also convinced that if men invested half as much emotion into their marriages, divorce rates would plummet, the contraceptive industry would boom, and the violent mood swings that characterize female behavior would cease almost entirely.

Even those of us whose wives support us by supplying the chips, dip, and soda during our weekend-long infatuation with the television must realize the toll sporting events take on our marriages and families. It can't be healthy when a man's first reaction in a moment of bitter defeat is to hit someone or something while the wife and kids are in the house. I've never allowed my disappointment to lead to domestic violence, but I've found myself lacking patience when interacting with my family in the aftermath of a loss. Watching my team lose does nothing to make me a better husband or father.

Am I suggesting that men give up sports? Not necessarily.

But it does seem that we should perhaps redirect some of the energy and emotion we invest in sports into our marriages. So one day when your wife returns from the store with the pretzels and peanuts to replenish the stock that will sustain you during your withdrawal into the world of sports, surprise her by suggesting that the two of you skip the big game and go to dinner instead. Or rent a classic chick flick, pop some popcorn, and curl up on the couch together. Tell her you'd rather go out with her than watch the game (even if you might be stretching the truth).

You don't need to skip every game, but your wife will appreciate the gesture, particularly if she knows how much a particular game means to you. At the very least, she'll be relieved that she won't have to endure another tirade. And spending the evening with your wife will ultimately prove a better and more beneficial place to channel your emotions.

sixteen

In Good Company:
Star Gazing

I took a chance on my first date with the woman I would later marry. No, I played the part of the perfect gentleman. I didn't even attempt a first-date kiss. Rather, I took her to a football game.

Such a move proved risky in several respects. Perhaps she didn't like football. But more crucially, driving time between her house and the stadium exceeded an hour and a half. We had only talked briefly prior to the date, so I hoped—indeed, prayed—that the conversation wouldn't lag. I'm a fairly talkative person, but could I keep up the chatter for an hour-and-a-half drive, through a football game she might not be interested in, and then for another hour-and-a-half drive going home? Surely I was putting myself in a precarious position.

Even if I held up my end of the conversation, there were no guarantees she would do the same. What if she proved to be a dud, a nontalker? What if the level of conversation dipped painfully low? Frankly, I've had more enlightening conversations with two-year-olds than I've had with some dates.

To ease my anxieties, I prepared a mental list of topics: family, interests, hobbies. The usual stuff. In the event we exhausted these topics, I prepared a number of backup questions designed to really get to know my date: If you could be anyone in the history of the world for a day, who would you be and why? If given an airline ticket to any place on the planet, where would you go? If empowered by the president of the United States to create a new national holiday, what and when would it be? I even anticipated questions she might ask me and rehearsed potential answers.

I didn't go to such extreme lengths with all my dates. At the time, this woman I would eventually marry seemed untouchable, well beyond the reach of a bloke like me. I merely wanted to make a good impression, prove that I was no dud myself. So close to the promised land, failure was not an option.

The pressure proved to be almost more than I could bear. Picking her up, I was wound so tight that even breathing became a challenge. And then something wonderful happened. After my first clumsy question, the conversation started and lasted the duration of our drive, through an entire football game, and the drive home. Our exchange proved free and easy, and I instantly forgot my list of questions and rehearsed responses. Her voice, her every word held me captive. I became unconscious of myself, my anxieties, and our words performed a symphony as grand and glorious as any performed at Carnegie Hall.

Not wanting to relinquish her company, I asked her to dinner and a late movie. She accepted. A date that began at 9

A.M. ended—without a kiss—at well after midnight, and never once did conversation wane.

In a year and a half of dating, I never tired of her company; indeed, I relished it. And I still do, although time to just sit and talk has been splintered by a career, a household, and children. It is tragically easy to let days go by without having a single meaningful conversation. By the time the kids are put to bed and the house put back in order, we often are too tired to talk.

To continue the symphony started more than twelve years ago, we now have to consciously create talktime, and I've found that a perfect venue for this is under a canopy of stars. After we've put the kids to bed, I grab a blanket and my wife, and we take refuge on the backyard lawn. Or I get a babysitter, and we head to a park or some other secluded spot. The object is to find some place quiet where we can focus on each other and remember how much we enjoy the other's company.

seventeen

The Choices We Make:

Ladies' Night Out

I recently faced one of those dilemmas that plague men throughout their married lives. I was just leaving the office when the phone rang. It was my best friend from high school, and he had tickets to a Utah Jazz basketball game. A night of NBA action! Slam dunks! Food and drink! Seems like a no-brainer, right? I go to the game.

Well, it wasn't that easy. It was the first Wednesday of the month. That meant Ladies' Night Out, a monthly ritual I wholeheartedly endorse. Indeed, I was thrilled when my wife and her friends organized what one of the other husbands regretfully referred to as a women's liberation movement sweeping the neighborhood.

This man, not nearly the freethinker I am, felt as if he was losing control. Sure, he went fishing almost every weekend with his buddies, leaving his wife and kids alone at home. That, after all, is the natural order of things, right? Men work hard all week and need some rest and relaxation on the weekends. Now he was stuck home with his kids one night a month. Oh the inhumanity! Not the kids!

I tried to explain that a night out would do both his wife and their marriage good. A night out might result in less frequent mood swings. Our wives needed a break from time to time, I reasoned.

He agreed that they needed a break, but did he have to stay home alone with the kids? Couldn't the wives take the kids with them? He shivered at the mere possibility. For him, Ladies Night Out was a sentence, like being condemned to the lions' den.

I then realized I needed to argue in a language he could understand. I said, "The real issue here is what's in it for us" (as if our wives' happiness wasn't enough). His face went blank. Clearly, he still couldn't see past the horrors of child care.

"Look at Ladies Night Out as an investment," I explained. He needed to realize that there was the possibility of a return, a kickback. There was a chance that his wife might rediscover her passion for him while he was home taming the kids.

I now had his attention. At the very least, Ladies' Night Out alleviates some of the guilt we men feel when we recognize just how good we've got it. Even the most unconscionable man knows in his gut that the ratio of Men's to Ladies' Nights Out is overwhelmingly in our favor. That one night out makes approaching our wives about a weekend golf excursion or a night out with the boys a heck of a lot easier.

As a relatively enlightened husband who prides himself on his selflessness, I immediately declined my friend's invitation to watch the Jazz, choosing my wife's happiness over a mere basketball game. But then came the irresistible blow. "They're luxury box seats," he said.

With that statement, he may as well have been the serpent in Eden or the sirens that seduced Ulysses and his men. To resist was futile. How could I turn down seats to a Jazz game in a fully catered luxury suite? I couldn't. Such an act was beyond the strength of any mortal man.

And what made the forbidden fruit even more tantalizing is that I knew my wife would change her plans for me. Of course, I knew going to the game would ultimately cost me in one way or another. She wouldn't give up Ladies' Night Out for nothing.

Deep down, I knew the right thing to do was to decline my friend's invitation, stay home with the kids, and let my wife enjoy her night out. Surely my wife's happiness was more important than satisfying my own desires. But seats in a luxury suite?

Like so many times before, I was faced with deciding between what I knew was right and what I wanted, and I cursed the gods for toying with me in such a cruel manner. And like so many times before, I naturally made the wrong decision, but in a sick and twisted sort of way, I don't regret it. The game was great. Sure, it cost me. As I left for the game that night, the last words I heard were: "You owe me big." And the next Saturday she gave me a honey-do list as long as our kids' Christmas-wish lists. Was it worth it? You bet your bottom it was. Come on. A luxury suite.

In the long run, I doubt I'll ever pay my wife back for the multitude of sacrifices she makes on my behalf, and it's unlikely that I'll ever match her selflessness. But that doesn't mean I shouldn't try, and she certainly needs a break from time to time. All wives and mothers do.

One easy way of providing your wife a few hours escape and giving back a little to her is to come home from work, assume responsibility for the kids, and tell her she can go and do whatever she'd like. You might even make arrangements for her to go out with a group of her friends—Ladies' Night Out initiated by men. How progressive! And you might even give her a credit card if your enlightened thinking borders on the radical.

eighteen

How to Tame a Hurricane on the Home Front:
The Gift Bag

The key to any gift given to one's wife is an attention to detail and the perceived thoughtfulness of the gift. This is particularly true of the gift bag.

While an attention to detail and thoughtfulness may be a stretch for the masculine mind, husbands need to think carefully about the organization and content of the bag. Most men, including myself, would be content with dropping a box of chocolates, a few daisies, and a sexy something-or-other into a brown paper bag and calling it good.

Unfortunately, this won't do. In the first place, the sexy something-or-other is too obviously for you and not your wife. In the second place, a brown paper bag is suited for school lunch and cheap liquor, not a present for your wife. And finally, there's no rationale for the selection and arrangement of the bag's contents.

You might be thinking, *Why does there need to be a rationale? Isn't the thought alone enough?* You would think so, but this kind of thinking exudes with male naïveté.

Imagine the scenario. Just before you leave work, your wife calls, not to say how much she loves you and looks forward to your coming home, but to tell you the thirty-seven awful things "your" kids have done during the course of the day. You immediately recognize that the woman you once would have traversed mountains to spend a mere five minutes with has been ravaged by motherhood and metamorphosed into a raging, emotionally charged creature who holds you personally responsible for her lot in life. Trembling, you set the phone down and stare blankly at the wall in front of you, wondering how to delay your trip home.

You think quickly: *How can I disarm the bomb before it blows?* The light bulb flashes and you smile triumphantly. *I'll get her some flowers. No, I'll shower her with an array of gifts, bombard her with my thoughtfulness. She'll be so overwhelmed that she'll quickly forget the misery of her day.*

Then you take a mental voyage into the land of make-believe: *She'll be so taken by my thoughtfulness that she's going to want me something fierce,* and you buy the sexy something-or-other, imagining how she'll be instantly transformed into a bundle of passionate womanhood by your consideration.

By the time you get home, you're so impressed with how good a husband you are that you forget that Hurricane Helen is just on the other side of the door. You saunter in, glide into the kitchen, and greet with a smile and a kiss the face that only a husband could love.

Before she can let loose her frustrations, you present her

with your offering. You lay it on the countertop as if it were an altar and the bag your humble sacrifice to the marriage gods.

Your wife gives the bag a look that simultaneously borders on skeptical and irritated and asks, "What's that?" With an all-too-confident smile, you reply, "Just a little something for you, darling."

She then pulls from the bag a box of red hots in the shape of little hearts, a bottle of perfume, a single rose, some chocolate, and the sexy something-or-other.

Holding the last item up, she looks at you and asks, "And just who in the world is this for?" You sense immediately your own transparency. She sees right through you and your good intentions. As you slink away, you realize from the mounting disgust on your wife's face that you've trivialized her experience and made light of her day.

Was I really so foolish as to think that my little offering would instantly transform my wife back into the delightful woman I married? Did I really believe she would race to put on the sexy something-or-other and beat me to the bedroom just because of a little perfume and some chocolate? The sad truth is that the answer to these questions is yes! Oh, foolish, pitiful little man.

I don't mean to suggest that a gift bag isn't a good idea in this particular case. Quite the contrary, a gift bag is a wonderful idea in such situations. However, as I mentioned before, the planning and execution of the bag is crucial, particularly when disarming an irritated wife.

The first thing you need to acknowledge and even believe, if possible, is that your wife has had a day that would destroy most mortal men.

If you can bring yourself to believe this fact, then acting with the right intentions, which is the second step, will be relatively easy. You must genuinely want to do something to make her day better, not because you dread the idea of going home to a raging woman or because you can't get the sexy something-or-other off your mind, but because her happiness is your priority.

Once you've established the proper mind-set—which, again, is crucial—then you're prepared to choose an appropriate bag and plan for its contents. Rather than the brown paper bag, I recommend an actual gift bag, one designed specifically for gift giving. You've seen such bags at Christmas. Your wife likely has used these bags for baby showers and birthday gifts for her closest girlfriends.

Yes, I'm talking about the bags with the tissue paper sticking out the top, and yes, you'll need tissue paper too. With any luck the bag and tissue will match, which will impress, perhaps even startle, your wife.

Of course, I realize that purchasing such a bag and tissue in public may compromise your masculinity, and you may feel a little funny in the checkout line. But if you've adopted the right mind-set, you'll be able to make the sacrifice.

In choosing the bag's contents, you need to plan carefully. A haphazard selection of this and that won't do. I recommend some kind of theme.

I must admit, however, that I stumbled onto this idea accidentally. The first bag I gave my wife was—quite unintentionally—color coordinated: my bag had a pink theme. I included a bottle of pink body lotion, a pink lady's razor, a scented candle that also happened to be pink, and some other, well, pink stuff. The marriage gods must have been smiling on me that day because I even picked a pink flowered bag and pink tissue.

With all that pink, you'd think I would have noticed, but it was my wife who brought it to my attention. She was genuinely impressed that I had so carefully planned the bag's contents.

I have since planned every bag around a controlling theme. One such theme is "Things My Wife Likes." I include a Dr. Pepper, a Twix candy bar, a CD of one of her favorite bands, and so forth. Going with the color-coordinated theme on another occasion, I put things that are purple into a purple bag since purple is my wife's favorite color. You could choose a holiday or vacation theme. You might have a date theme where you include movie tickets, a gift certificate to her favorite restaurant, a new outfit to wear, and more. In other words, the possibilities are endless.

The key is to exert enough thought into planning the bag's contents that your wife will immediately recognize that you didn't throw it together on a whim. Of course, you may actually throw it together on a whim, but you just don't want it to look as if you did. Ultimately, you want the bag to say that you care enough about your wife that you took the time to put it together as well as possible.

Once you select the items for the bag, carefully—and I emphasize carefully—organize the contents and tissue in as artistic a fashion as you are able. On my first try, I thought this would be a snap, but I soon realized that getting the tissue to fluff and stick up just the right way is like sculpting water—the paper went wherever I didn't want it to go.

I would also encourage you to do the arranging in the privacy of your car or office. If you dread the idea of being seen buying a gift bag and tissue, imagine how you'll feel arranging it in public. To do it right, you'll have to suck up your masculine pride and make the attempt. But again, if you are acting with the right intentions, you'll be able to do it—and do it better than you think.

nineteen

If It's Broke, Fix It:
A Carpet Picnic

I'm convinced that men possess a genetic predisposition for screwing up. This is particularly true when interacting with the women we love most. Even our best intentions uncannily go awry. When I was ten, I set fire to the microwave while preparing a surprise breakfast for my mom. How was I to know that metal pans aren't microwave safe?

Shortly after getting married, I surprised my wife by doing the laundry. I had no idea rayon needs to be dry-cleaned. A tongue-lashing and a new ninety-five-dollar outfit made sure that I haven't forgotten. As it turns out, the little tags on clothing do more than indicate front and back; they include washing instructions!

Experiences like these have caused me to ponder at great length why it is that men have a proclivity for unintentionally aggravating the women in our lives. I would like to blame it on the feminine psyche, the fact that they're a bit irrational, a tad hypersensitive, and impossible to please.

I've even wondered if there isn't something buried beneath our own psyches that accounts for our seemingly natural ability to incur a woman's wrath, perhaps some Freudian Oedipus thing. Do we unconsciously delight in feminine ranting? Was it really so bad the first time our mothers spanked us?

But then I wonder if it's this complicated. Could it be that mere stupidity is the real reason for our marital blunders?

Take my brother-in-law as an example. The day after bringing his wife and firstborn child home from the hospital, he spent the day cleaning a friend's house. The friend's wife was out of town, and he wanted to surprise her upon her return. While my brother-in-law scoured and scrubbed another woman's house, his own wife, alone with a new baby in a home in need of its own tidying, prepared herself a can of soup for lunch while making a list of ways she could make her husband miserable for months to come.

From my brother-in-law's point of view, he was doing a good deed, helping a friend in need. From my sister-in-law's point of view—and from the point of view of anyone with a grain of common sense—his behavior epitomized male stupidity and insensitivity. To this day, he still can't figure out why his wife has not forgiven him for his display of friendship, and she can't figure out why he's so dense.

But are men really this stupid? I'm sure our wives often think so. But I would suggest that the ease and frequency with which men commit marital blunders indicates that the problem does, in fact, cut deep, right into our DNA. We seem to have a genetic predisposition for committing one stupid act after another. Consider how even the most determined man will eventually goof. The only fool-proof solution would involve slipping into a catatonic state—a state in which we don't act, think, or speak.

The best advice is to accept a cold, hard fact: men are an evolutionary mess. We screw up; it's inevitable. Sure, we would like to blame the marital discord that results from our mistakes on the bundles of irrational emotion we married, but we ultimately bring the sting of feminine displeasure on our own heads.

Facing the inevitability of our fate—prone to messing up and married to women acutely attuned to our insensitivity—it would seem that progress is antithetical to the whole marriage project. Or is it?

Once we've accepted the reality of our situation, we can turn our attention to doing those things that will restore us to the good graces of the women we love. Our disease cannot be cured, but it can be treated.

One possible treatment involves the element of surprise. And since we regularly surprise our wives with our insensitivity, surprising them with an act of thoughtfulness can be achieved rather easily. In fact, the real danger here is shocking our wives into a state of prolonged breathlessness or even inducing a heart attack.

To test my theory, just try doing the dishes or taking out the garbage without being asked. My wife still hasn't fully recovered from the first time I voluntarily cleaned the bathroom, including the toilet.

A slightly more elaborate surprise involves a blanket, candles, some chocolate-dipped strawberries, cheese and crackers, a bottle of your favorite romantic beverage, and some soft music. After spreading the blanket on the floor of a spacious room in your home, carefully and thoughtfully arrange the other items while your wife is either out of the house, putting the kids to bed, or taking a bath. In other words, the carpet picnic should come as a surprise. And if you've recently committed a potentially fatal error in judgment . . . perhaps inadvertently using one of your wife's finer dish towels to wipe your hands after changing the oil in her car—another good intention gone awry—a carpet picnic may be just what's needed to deflect her wrath and restore you to her good graces.

twenty

Shopping as Therapy:
The Surprise Shopping Day

There is much to the feminine psyche that most men, including myself, don't pretend to comprehend. Take, for example, a woman's coping mechanisms.

Not long after my wife and I were married, I returned home from a college class to find my new bride curled in the fetal position on the floor of our one-bedroom apartment. Strewn around her were the remains of an ice cream carton—Neapolitan, if I remember correctly—a half-dozen or so tear-stained tissues, and a half-empty two-liter bottle of Dr. Pepper.

When we parted company earlier that morning, she seemed fine, even upbeat. We had just moved into our apartment in a new town to begin graduate school, and she had been eager and excited to look for a job. What rested on the floor before me was the withered remains of her optimism. The job hunt hadn't gone so well.

As I eased into the role of sympathetic husband, cradling my infantlike wife in my arms, she sobbed, "No one likes me here. I want to go home."

"But it's only been one day; give it a chance."

Inwardly I was thinking, *Get a grip, woman!*

My next act was as disastrous as revealing what I was thinking. I began suggesting remedies to her problem, exploring potential options, and quizzing her on her day's efforts. The way I saw it, there was a problem and there certainly was a solution, and I foolishly thought my efforts to fix her problem would cure her depression.

With every suggestion, every encouraging word, however, she cried still harder, until, out of utter frustration, I cried out, "For gracious sake, woman, get a grip!"

A few more years of marriage taught me that, in such situations, my wife isn't looking for a fix to her problems. In fact, in the case of her job-hunting woes, my wife's journey into the depths of self-pity proved to be an effective fix in itself. The next day, after a flood of tears, a half-gallon of ice cream, and some soda pop, she eagerly arose from bed, left the apartment with determination, and returned with a job.

"See, I knew you'd do it," I said when I saw the smile on her face. Of course, my miscalculated comment immediately reminded her of how I had merely aggravated the situation the previous day, and what should have been an evening of celebration turned into one of those conversations in which she explains the intricacies of her emotions and I think to myself, *I don't get it.*

Now when I come home to find my wife curled up on the floor, I check the freezer for our supply of ice cream, curl up next to her, and bite my tongue. I've found it's better to descend into the enigmatic depths of her emotions with her than to offer quick fixes to her problems. I'm still befuddled by her coping mechanism, but at least my current protocol generally keeps the peace in our marriage.

Another of my wife's coping strategies involves shopping. While I initially found this strategy as perplexing as her wallows in self-pity, I've come to appreciate and understand it more the longer we've been married. Surprisingly, shopping has a lot in common with one of my own coping mechanisms.

When I'm a degree or two from overheating, I turn to the landscape—specifically, well-manicured greens and fairways. Not that I find the golf course a particularly peaceful place. With a twenty-plus handicap, I generally find more frustration on the course than I do rest and relaxation.

But even in the midst of a triple boggy, I remind myself that golf beats working. And if nothing else, the triple boggy allows me to redirect my hostility in such a way that the only things that pay the price for my frustrations are the few inanimate objects I beat with my clubs. No one is hurt or offended by my tantrums or profane exclamations, not even my playing partner, who understands completely the agony I'm experiencing. In the end, I always feel a little better after even the most aggravating round of golf.

My wife, on the other hand, finds peace and serenity in the hustle and bustle of shopping. Even roaming the mall on the busiest of shopping days brings a satisfied smile to her face. Indeed, there seems to be something therapeutic in a seemingly aimless trek through her favorite department store. Not looking for anything in particular, she will scour every rack without breaking a sweat. And the success of her trip isn't measured by the number of bags she brings home. Occasionally, and to my relief, she comes home empty-handed.

As with me on the golf course, there is, for my wife, no such thing as a bad day shopping, and she inevitably returns from her trips a little happier than when she left.

Unfortunately, I can't afford to golf every day. But an occasional round, I've discovered, is a necessary expense, and while it's taken me a long time to acknowledge it, shopping is likewise a necessary expense. My wife's mental health depends on it.

As a man, you certainly can imagine how delighted you'd be if, one Saturday morning, you awoke, anticipating a day of yard work, and found that your wife had made a tee time and had even loaded your clubs in the trunk of the car. Imagine how excited your wife would be to awake to a day of shopping instead of domestic drudgery.

While most men don't have a problem taking time off work for eighteen holes of golf, I suspect most would be reluctant to take a day off to stay home and watch the kids while their wives go shopping. But if we recognize that shopping actually makes our wives more happy and more pleasant, we might be more eager to encourage their efforts.

And I suggest making this shopping day a surprise. Perhaps even arrange to have her closest shopping partner meet her at the mall. Or consider getting a babysitter and going shopping with her. Of course, this requires a certain degree of fortitude since a single complaint on your part will ruin the day for her. And be willing to bite the bullet on another matter: give her the credit card. She might even buy a little something for you at the sporting goods store or, better yet, Victoria's Secret.

TWENTY-
one

"How Do I Love Thee?":
A Passionate Love Letter

One of the beauties of love is its power to blind and befuddle the mind.

If it weren't for the intoxicating powers of love, I'm not sure I could have ever convinced my wife to marry me. Given the outrageous flaws in my personality and my countless shortcomings, my wife was surely out of her mind when she said "yes" to my marriage proposal. And what's even more amazing is that she continues to love me even after marriage!

During courtship, I successfully disguised and otherwise

concealed a variety of imperfections that have since been exposed by the penetrating light of married life. Kept a close secret while dating, my bathroom rituals alone, too personal to be discussed in detail here, are enough to ward off any sane woman. Yet I perform these rituals on a daily basis in full view of the woman I love. And here's the kicker: she still finds me desirable on occasion.

This realization raises a perplexing question: How is it I can remain a prince charming of sorts in the eyes of someone who sees clearly and regularly the ogre in me? The answer? Love. Without it I doubt seriously that any man could convince a woman to spend her life with him.

If we men understood this simple truth, we might be less self-conscious about expressing our love for our wives. Unfortunately, most of us are more eloquent in our casual conversations with other men than we are in expressing our feelings for our wives. I suppose that our anxiety regarding our ability to articulate our innermost feelings accounts for this paradox.

And if we're afraid to vocalize our feelings, we're far more reluctant to write them down. At least the verbal utterance is fleeting and disappears into thin air the moment it escapes our lips. The written word is much more permanent. What if someone other than our wives were to get hold of our sappy ramblings? Worse yet, what if our most sincere, heartfelt words come across as so silly and inane that even our wives can't contain their laughter? If our words are written down, there's no denying that they are ours.

But thanks to that hallucinogenic drug called love, we need not worry about our wives mocking our expressive efforts. So long as we act with sincerity, I suspect that the most mushy, even pathetic love letter will stir the heart of a woman in love. My wife certainly looks past more glaring defects than my clumsy expressions of the heart.

So let loose. Write your wife the most heartfelt love letter. Tell her you love her in as many ways and in as many metaphors as you can conjure up. Tell her your love runs as deep as the deepest ocean, is as constant as the flow of traffic on a busy highway, and is stronger than the smell of fresh-made cheese. Tell her that being apart is worse than Christmas without Santa Claus. Or take the simple, straight-forward approach and just say, "I love you."

I recommend using some fine stationery, something with flowers or embroidery, and writing in your finest hand. You might even use a quill and ink. Then put the letter some place unexpected—in the fridge or a kitchen drawer. Attach it to the steering wheel of her car. Send it to her in the mail. Just put it somewhere where she'll be sure to get it and be surprised. Oh, and be sure you put it in a place where no one else will find it since what will draw a sigh from your wife may draw smirks or even uncontrollable laughter from anyone else.

two

Friends and Marriage:
A Weekend Getaway with a Friend

Courtship and married life are mired in ironic twists and grand paradoxes. Consider, for example, how courtship and marriage influence your relationships with your male friends.

While dating the woman you would someday marry, you likely abandoned your friends to spend every possible minute you could with her. And if your friends did not have girlfriends themselves, they saw your undying devotion as a sign of weakness. You were, in their eyes, hopelessly and pathetically whipped.

Even though you recognized, as did your friends, that they inwardly longed for what you had—wanting in the deepest, most-remote corners of their souls to be likewise whipped—you felt, at times, a degree of shame for your constancy and devotion.

Then, on Saturday nights, holding the woman you loved in your arms and realizing your friends were, at that exact moment, sitting in somebody's basement watching reruns of past Super Bowls, all the while wishing they were in your shoes, you thanked God. On bended knee, you acknowledged His graciousness in making your Saturday nights more meaningful and rewarding.

Even on those rare occasions when you weren't with your girlfriend, you avoided your friends at all costs, knowing full well the ridicule, the merciless verbal abuse you would be subjected to for your constant devotion to a member of the opposite sex. Even though you knew that each jeering word was tainted by your friends' hypocrisy, you accepted that such constancy to a woman essentially amounted to a symbolic emasculation, a loss of some intangible part of your manhood.

But by abandoning your friends and past Super Bowls, you paradoxically found a feature of your masculinity buried beneath the rugged exterior of male bravado. You discovered refinement, sensitivity, and the warm fuzzies associated with love. You suddenly realized that you were capable of speaking without the aid of colorful expletives; you discovered that there's more to women than designer jeans and swimsuits; and you learned in a revelatory flash that romance can be as thrilling as a game-winning field goal. You not only came to appreciate chick flicks, but you joyfully participated in the cathartic release of emotions elicited by each sentimental ending. And you came to accept a brutal truth: your friends had to be abandoned for a greater good.

And then, just days after the honeymoon, you made another, equally paramount discovery: you missed your male friends. From that moment on, you looked for every opportunity to momentarily escape the marriage noose and rekindle those relationships strained by months, perhaps even years of courtship.

I'm not so sure that our desire to golf isn't driven more by our inherent need for male bonding than it is by the love of the game.

I'm not suggesting that our love for our wives diminishes after marriage, or that we no longer prefer their company to our friends. It's just that we find something in our shared experiences as husbands, fathers, and men that, paradoxically, makes us better husbands, fathers, and men.

I'm convinced that if I golf at least once a week or go on an occasional weekend fishing trip with a buddy or two, I return to my wife and children a better man. Perhaps those few hours or days in the company of men allow me to regress a bit and let loose that part of my masculinity necessarily repressed by marriage. Perhaps those few hours or days serve to remind me how fortunate I am to be married to a wonderful woman. For whatever reason, I believe that time off to be in the company of other men is essential to my own mental health and the health of my marriage.

If there's any truth in this proposition, then it stands to reason that that same principle applies to our wives. Certainly they need time off to be with their friends, although, for them, time off isn't always as easily achieved as it is for us. With raising children and maintaining a household, my wife spends far less time in the company of her friends than I do in the company of mine.

This is unfortunate since women seem to benefit as much, if not more, from time off with their friends. My wife always returns from a shopping or lunch trip with her best friend a little less stressed than she was before and a lot more happy. Early in our marriage, I suspect I was a little jealous of my wife's friend for having this effect. I've since realized that her friends, like mine, fill an emotional need that only friends are capable of filling.

Given this fact, as well as the difficulty most women have

breaking free of their families, I recommend sending your wife away on an occasional weekend getaway with her best friend or a group of friends.

To ensure that she makes the trip, you might plan it yourself with your wife's friend and then spring it on your wife as a surprise. Imagine her delight when she discovers that you're sending her to a spa for the weekend, or a quaint resort community for a few days of rest and relaxation. I'm not so sure the place is as nearly as important as the company and just providing your wife with some time off with her friends.

Of course, this means you'll have to manage the home front, and it's imperative that your wife return from her weekend to an orderly house. If she walks into the apocalypse—screaming kids, dirty dishes, and laundry strewn from wall to wall—the desirable effects of her excursion will instantly fade. If you have to hire professional cleaners, do it. Just make sure her return doesn't bring a screeching halt to her vacation.

TWENTY-
three

Getting and Spending:
A Cash Prize

Although the financial demands of contemporary society often press both husband and wife into the workforce, the more traditional arrangement of man as provider and woman as homemaker was undoubtedly motivated by sound economic principles. Indeed, I would go so far as to argue that the move from a feudal to a market-driven economy necessitated bread-winners as well as breadspenders.

Under the old feudal system, women worked even harder than they do now. They raised children, spun wool, churned butter, milked cows, manufactured candles, concocted medicinal ointments, bottled fruits and vegetables, and even helped with the plowing of fields and the harvesting of crops. Without the local supermarket, women's work involved the production of life's necessities, in addition to all it entails today.

Fortunately or not, capitalism gave way to affordable manufactured goods: clothing, dairy products, medicines, and produce could be purchased in the marketplace. Men left their farms for factories and businesses, stranding their wives at home contemplating a new use for the butter churn. To the delight of one industrious female pioneer—a premodern Martha Stewert—the old churn made a fine flowerpot.

There was, however, a downside to the new system. Once the butter churn had been converted into a piece of household decor, wives were left with an unusual amount of time on their hands. For the first time in human history, the concept of leisure developed among the middle-class masses. Sure, the children still needed to be cared for and some household duties attended to, but relatively speaking, women were left to themselves. I suspect that public education became popular at about this same time, thereby relieving women of one of their few remaining strenuous duties—raising kids.

With their husbands and children out of the house, women faced the challenge of filling their days. They had, of course, several options: hard liquor, regular chats with neighboring women, naps, reading, and with the invention of television, daytime talk shows and *Days of Our Lives*. The experience with the butter churn also convinced them that any tangible object could, with a little imagination and ingenuity, be transformed into a decorative household item. Thus sprung Pampered Chef parties, gossip, romance novels, an infatuation with chocolate, and a hundred and one uses for a coffee can. While such activities kept women housebound for a number of years, housewives eventually grew restless. A craft away from completely losing their collective minds, women turned to the marketplace, not as producers but as consumers of manufactured goods.

Shopping as a mode of feminine behavior was born, and from the imagination of a shrewd and enterprising businessman came the invention of the mall. From that day forward, women roamed the department stores in packs and herds, seeking with a dogged determination every sale and bargain imaginable.

Men would call home during the day only to discover that their wives had changed their daytime residence to Sears or Nordstrom's. As men watched their checking accounts shrink and their credit card debt grow exponentially, they quickly grew leery of this new thing called shopping. *Surely there must be a cheaper way to spend time*, they wondered. Men even began racking their brains for a hundred and two things their wives could do with a coffee can. But it was too late. Men were forced to confront what seemed a hard reality: their wives had learned to spend with precision and completeness their hard-earned money.

But what most men failed to realize then and fail to realize today is that their wives are actually providing a necessary service by frequenting the mall-ways of America. Ours is a consumer society that depends on the circulation of the all-mighty dollar. If it were left up to most men, I suspect not too many dollars would circulate. We would hoard and save and save and hoard until the economy imploded.

Thanks to the spending habits of our wives, we live in a country with the most vibrant economy in the world. We should praise, not curse, their willingness, indeed, their eagerness, to spend our hard-earned cash, and the man who founded the mall, so often vilified amongst men, should be praised for providing in one location a place of habitation for our wives.

Given the economic necessity of shopping as well as our wives' love affair with it, we would do well to provide them with the resources needed to make their contribution to the gross national product. While they will likely spend with or without our consent, women do, in fact, appreciate it when we encourage their spending habits, and secretly setting aside a little money each month and then surprising your wife with a chunk of cash to spend in whatever way she sees fit is certainly a worthwhile gesture.

Whether ten dollars or a thousand, she will appreciate your consideration, especially if you put some thought into how you present her with her cash prize. You might hide it in a place she'll find it or even send her on a scavenger hunt. You might present it to her as part of a romantic dinner, or send it in the mail in a nice, perhaps even handmade card (see chapter 13). Not only will you make her happy, but you'll also be doing your part to keep the national economy moving in a positive direction.

four

Men's Work and Women's Work:
A Scavenger Hunt

At a certain point in most women's lives, particularly in the lives of those women who choose to stay home with their children, the average day degenerates into a hectic routine that would drive the average man to madness. I'm convinced that the reason men are traditionally the breadwinners in most households is because a job serves as a viable escape from the pandemonium of the home.

Our earliest ancestral males recognized immediately the extreme hardship of rearing children and maintaining an orderly household. When it came time to determine who would be the hunter-gatherers, I imagine the men eagerly volunteered.

They naturally embraced the opportunity to flee the ceaseless crying, the smelly squirrel-skin diapers, and the endless cycle of cleaning necessitated by the children's endless cycle of mess making. I suspect that the whole concept of hunting and gathering was devised by a group of men seeking sanctuary, a place remote and distant from the tumult of the home.

Imagine this group of men huddled around a small fire, contemplating their options. One, we'll call him Stig, suggests that they abandon the women and children altogether. Strike out on their own, he argues, create a civilization of men, devoid of crying fits and nagging.

Of course, Stig isn't the sharpest spear in the quiver, and his proposal takes an immediate hit when no one volunteers to do the cooking and cleaning. The final blow comes when Mak, one of the perkier men in the bunch, suggests that a society without women, while certainly less prone to violent mood swings, would degenerate into a society of uptight men who would be driven to extreme outlets for their pent-up needs.

Gort, one of the more cunning in the group, then makes another proposal. What if they devise a way of escaping the drudgeries of domestic life, perhaps on a daily basis, without fully abandoning the women and children. Perhaps something could draw them away for hours and, occasionally, days at a time. Of course, they would have to convince their women that they were performing a needed and vital service. Indeed, this work would be essential to the survival of their families and civilization. This work would get them out of the cave for the greater part of a day, yet it would still afford them the benefits of a clean cave, a hot meal, and a warm bed.

And if they pitched the idea just right, they could convince their mates that they—the women—were somehow obligated to perform their domestic duties as a sign of gratitude for the work the men performed for their benefit. Thus, the concept of men's work and women's work was born.

While the men enthusiastically embrace Gort's proposal and herald him as *the Man*, a group of women are, of course, huddled around a fire at the opposite end of the cave wondering how they can get rid of their men, not permanently, since they perform a few tasks essential to the survival of the species, but intermittently and for substantial periods of time.

Though they regard their men with a certain degree of affection, the thought of spending all day, every day in the same cave causes even the most steady of women to shudder in horror. The work of cleaning and caring for the young is tough, they admit, but it's certainly easier without the help of a bungling man whose bouts with orneriness merely contribute to the chaos of the cave.

Hence, they welcome Gort's proposal, recognizing that if they accept primary responsibility for their children and households, their men will be under obligation to them. When the men return from hunting and gathering—certainly less arduous work than raising children—they'll feel compelled to assume some responsibility for the cooking, cleaning, and rearing, thus supplying them—the women—with an occasional break from their labors. Thus, one of the great ironies of married life was born.

And even now, thousands of years later, I'm sure there are days when my wife is as eager to see me leave for work as I am to go to work. But I'd like to think that we've become more enlightened with the evolution of our species—if not collectively than at least individually.

The fact that the most appealing aspect of my job on some days is that it gets me out of the house should send a clear message that my wife works hard, probably harder than I do. Unfortunately for her, she is often housebound.

Hence, creating opportunities for her to escape the drudgeries of domestic life is something she generally appreciates. One way of doing this is to send her on a scavenger hunt—appropriate, since I've been talking about hunting and gathering.

No, I'm not suggesting that you send your wife to the

neighbors looking for a burned match and a used turkey thermometer. Rather, begin the hunt by sending her a dozen roses with a note instructing her to wind her way to a local spa for a professional massage. Have the masseuse give her another note directing her to her favorite beautician, where she can have her hair done and receive a manicure. You might include a small gift bag (see chapter 18) with her favorite magazine, a beverage, and a snack to enjoy during her visit.

The next note, included in the bag, could then send her to lunch. You might make arrangements for her best friend to meet her there. This wins points in a couple of ways: one, your wife will enjoy the surprise opportunity to see her friend; and two, you know darn well that the friend is going to go on about how she wished her husband were more like you (see chapter 7).

After lunch, your wife's friend can give her a note directing her to the mall and a women's apparel store, where you've instructed the clerk to help your wife choose a new dress or outfit for dinner. All of this, of course, needs to be prepaid. From there, you can have your wife meet you at a fine restaurant or even at a hotel room, where room service is waiting.

Of course, the possibilities of places to send your wife on her hunt are endless. You certainly can come up with less elaborate and expensive hunts. Perhaps you can devise a series of love notes or a progressive picnic. At each stop your wife could collect appetizers, an entrée, and some dessert, eventually ending up at a secluded park, where you await her arrival. The key, I think, is to just get her out of the house for a while. And don't forget to make arrangements for the kids.

TWENTY-
five

Talk Is Cheap:
Real Love and a Profound Sacrifice

I like to deer hunt. Not because I necessarily enjoy killing other living creatures, although there is something to be said about stalking an illusive prey. Indeed, the parallels between big game hunting and courtship may account for the instinctive impulse men have for both activities.

I enjoy hunting for a variety of other reasons. Being in the outdoors, bonding with my brothers and father, and swapping stories of past hunts make the experience both communal and ritualistic.

To me, the kill hardly represents the best part of the hunt. Not even close. Looking back, I certainly recall with distinct vividness the first deer I ever shot. But I remember with even more vividness hearing my dad let slip a truly monumental expletive for the first time. Sure, I'd heard him bark out an occasional heck or darn while growing up, but he generally exercised restraint—at least until one memorable deer hunt.

On this hunt, my father devised an elaborate plan of attack to hunt an especially rugged canyon. My brothers and I were each given specific responsibilities. My older brother would work up one side of the canyon, I would take the middle, and my father, along with my younger brother, would work up the far side. The idea was to push deer into a position where one of us could get a shot. My dad's orders were to move at a slow but steady pace and eventually meet up at a designated point up the canyon.

An easy enough plan, right? About halfway into the plan, my brother and I lost patience. We hadn't seen any deer and we both were tired. Out of sight of my dad, we decided to abandon the plan altogether and beeline it for the truck. En route, we spotted an unsuspecting squirrel, and unable to resist, we both let lose with a shot. Both shots missed their mark, thereby confirming our decision to become *big* game hunters. Neither of us gave much thought to the fact that my dad most certainly heard our shots and assumed we were shooting at deer.

When we got to the truck, we cracked open a soda, leaned back against a tree, and waited. About two hours later, my dad, red in the face and sweating profusely, came into view. After beating the bush and looking and waiting for us, not knowing if we'd downed a deer or had wandered off and gotten lost, he cut to the chase: "What in the heck happened to you two?"

"Well," we explained feebly, "we weren't seeing any deer and we . . . well, we decided to come back to the truck and . . . well, there was this squirrel and we bet the other he couldn't hit it and . . ."

Our explanation didn't exactly prove a satisfactory response.

Instead, it confirmed his suspicions. And then it came with the grace and eloquence that only truck drivers and lumberjacks can appreciate: "Darn it, boys, when we decide on a *#@*!/> plan, you stick to it!"

Our mouths dropped in disbelief but only for a moment. In the next instant, my eyes met my brothers and we both smiled and burst into laughter, an unusual response given this was as angry as we'd ever seen our father. My dad was as startled by our reaction as we were by his eloquence, and even he cracked a smile. Oh, he was still mad as Hades, but something much more profound than anger had happened.

For the first time in my life, I saw my dad in a different light. In that one utterance, he descended from the lofty heights of fatherhood and became human. He was a man, as fallible as any. And that one profane word seemed to signal that he saw us as men too. We were no longer merely father and sons. We were friends with no hierarchies dividing us. We were on common ground. For my brothers and myself, it was a rite of passage. Our father had spoken to us in the common language of men.

Our hunts have never been the same. While hunting, we are all men and the best of friends. We talk in ways and about topics that are beyond the bounds of civil family life, and while our wives would likely view the change as degenerative, no experience I can think of has brought us closer together.

What does all this have to do with marriage and making the wife happy? I share this experience to illustrate how important the deer hunt is to me. In fact, my wife might say that it's more important to me than our marriage. I disagree, but if my wife insisted that I make a choice between the two, say, by bagging the deer hunt to spend the weekend with her, I would admittedly struggle with the decision. Not because I'd rather deer hunt than be with my wife. No, like most men, I want it all.

I want to be able to golf, hunt, fish, hang out with the guys, spend time with the family, spend time with my wife, and so forth. I'm reluctant to give up anything if I can help it. Rather than give up the hunt, I would suggest that she come along or that we spend a different weekend together.

I've come to learn, however, that I'd be missing the point of my wife's ultimatum. She knows how much deer hunting means to me. She even supports me in this endeavor, despite her serious reservations regarding the ethicality of hunting.

By posing what even she realizes would be a difficult decision for me, she would really be probing the depth of my love. Would I be willing to give up hunting *for her,* even for a mere weekend? Spending the weekend with her would provide the most emphatic proof that my love is boundless.

To my female readers, the choice seems a no-brainer. In fact, they probably think I'm a heel of a husband for wrestling with what seems the obvious choice. But my male readers understand completely the severity of my situation. We don't like to make these kinds of choices. We frequently ask ourselves, "Why can't I love my wife and still golf every other day?" We strenuously believe in our capacity to do so.

What I've realized, however, is that our wives really don't want us to give up golf or hunting. What they want is proof: hard evidence that we love them more than all of our hobbies combined. One way of demonstrating our love is to make a supreme sacrifice, like choosing a weekend together as opposed to a hunting trip. Yes, we have to be willing to give something up on occasion. As my wife puts it, "Talk is cheap. Don't tell me you love me. Show me."

TWENTY-
SIX

Mamma's Boys:
Find a Fault and Fix It

I'm a bit of a mamma's boy. I admit it. I think most men are to a certain extent. Who can blame us? Mothers coddle their boys, and mine was no exception. My mother operated from the assumption that my brothers and I, unlike her more independent daughter, were incapable of taking care of ourselves, and she was generally right.

As I've grown older, I've come to appreciate my mother's ceaseless efforts to ensure my well-being and happiness. But when I was younger, I admittedly took her for granted. I lived in a world wherein beds were magically made, dirty laundry cleaned and pressed itself, and meals emerged from the kitchen instantaneously upon request. I gave little thought to one of the great mysteries of daily life—how I could leave a room in total disarray and return hours, perhaps only minutes later, to a room completely cleansed of my sloppiness. Despite my most concerted efforts, the rooms I cluttered seemed to spontaneously renew themselves on a daily basis. This renewal was, for me, part of the natural order of things, like the rotation of the earth or the rising and setting of the sun. I was oblivious to the drudgeries of domestic life.

My mother's coddling did not stop with her unflagging attention to my physical needs. She was equally attuned to my emotional well-being, and any time my self-esteem took a hit, she was always there to nurse my wounds.

Most important, my mother's love blinded her to my faults, a motherly attribute that, during my adolescent years, proved a formidable ally. In my mother's eyes, I was an infallible creature—"the golden child," as my wife laments. I can't count how many times my mother's delusions of sonly grandeur rescued me from the wrath of an angry father.

After I had carelessly backed over the neighbor's mailbox in my parents' new car, my mother convinced my dad (and me) that it wasn't possibly my fault. The neighbors had clearly made a poor choice in placing their mailbox, and if my father had let her, my mother would have insisted that the neighbors pay for damages.

After I got caught committing an unmentionable crime, she blamed my best friend. "Danny made him do it," she exclaimed. Indeed, anytime Danny and I did anything at all naughty, my mother couldn't bring herself to believe that I was a willing participant. I suspect that the only reason she allowed me to run around with Danny at all was her unwavering faith that my goodness would rub off. Surely she had an obligation to allow her noble son to rescue a wayward youth from a life of crime and degeneracy.

Of course, I allowed my mother to indulge her fantasies, and I even convinced myself that I was, in fact, the golden child. I was destined for greatness, fated to leave a profound impression on the history of the human species.

Then I got married, and my own deluded world collided with the windshield of reality. I learned in an instant that I was far from perfect.

Not that my wife didn't see the best in me. Obviously she saw something that merited her hand in marriage. But from day one of our marriage, she didn't allow herself to be duped by my few good qualities, nor has my mother, despite intense efforts, been able to convince her that I am the golden child. To my mother, I'm a Greek god; to my wife, a mere mortal, albeit one with some above-average qualities but one who is inevitably prone to errors in judgment.

Another way of looking at the situation is to say that my mother sees me as finished, my wife as a work in progress. And while the two get along well enough, their competing visions of the man they both love have created a bit of tension in our relationships.

Shortly after my wife and I were married, my mother called to see what my wife had made for dinner. "Brett works hard, you know, and he needs a good meal when he gets home," she explained.

Slightly annoyed, my wife rehearsed this conversation to me. I couldn't figure out why she was so irritated. Surely she recognized that I worked hard, that I returned from work hungry.

And why did my wife seem so put out when my mother would visit and inspect every nook and cranny of our apartment? Instinctively, my mom would find something to clean. *Great*, I thought. Not only had meals ceased to instantaneously appear since I got married, but I quickly noticed that my messes lingered for days. Indeed, for the first time in my life, I was confronted with a frightening reality: if I didn't clean up after myself, who would? Me? A novel idea but one I was hardly willing to accept.

If my mother paid a visit and felt inclined to clean up after her son, why not let her?

To my wife, such behavior was inexcusable, a breach of common courtesy, and an invasion of privacy. Our apartment was our space, not my mother's.

All this is to say that I've since had to cut the cord, although my wife thinks that, if anything, I've just stretched it a bit. And part of me really doesn't mind cutting the cord. Can I blame my wife for not wanting to live with someone who believes that messes clean themselves?

No, marriage has proven that I'm not nearly as perfect as my mother believes, and it shows me ways I can improve on a daily basis. I've learned that I can, in fact, clean up after myself. I've learned that the kitchen table isn't there to serve as a repository for my keys and briefcase. I've realized that I should spend less time yelling at the TV while watching a ball game and more time talking to my wife. I've even accepted the fact that leaving the room to break wind is a basic courtesy.

The point is, there are things I can do better; we all can do better. Our wives appreciate it when we do. So find a fault and fix it. If you're still deluded into believing that you are the golden child and can't identify a fault, ask your wife. She'll likely have a list all ready for you. The important thing is that you commit yourself to fixing the fault, and I would suggest announcing your intentions to your wife; you might even write down your intentions (see chapter 8). This way you'll have something to remind you of your commitment if you slack off.

TWENTY-
seven

There's No Fairness in Marriage:

Accept Responsibility,
Even When It's Not Your Fault

Early in my marriage, I came to the conclusion that there's
no such thing as fairness in marriage. The scales, I thought,
tipped overwhelmingly in my wife's favor, and I became convinced that, for our marriage to work, I was going to have
to make a disproportionate share of sacrifices. I reluctantly
accepted what seemed a cold, hard fact: I was solely responsible
for any disharmony in our relationship.

This revelation shook the foundations of my faith. I entered
into the marriage contract believing that, in most situations,

husbands and wives made mutual, though not necessarily equal, contributions to their marital tiffs. It was rare, I thought, for any one individual to be totally responsible for the disagreements and misunderstandings that disrupt moments of marital harmony.

Going in, I also knew full well that there would be times when, because of insensitivity and selfishness, I would justifiably incur the wrath of my wife, just as I believed that she too would commit her share of marital blunders.

What I perceived as balance or equilibrium in marriage made understanding and forgiveness essential ingredients for a successful marriage. I reasoned that my wife would look past my blunders as I looked past hers.

It only took a fight or two to upset many of these assumptions. I learned in a hurry that I could, in fact, be solely responsible for our marital strife. Indeed, even on occasions when I thought I occupied the moral high ground, my wife had an uncanny ability to gracefully turn my arguments against me. If I accused her of insensitivity on a particular occasion, she could immediately list with dates and in chronological order the countless times I had committed even more heinous infractions. After a while, she'd be in tears and I'd be making fervent apologies for my insensitivity.

I don't mean to imply here that my wife never accepts responsibility or never apologizes. One of her finest attributes is her willingness to say she's sorry. The catch is that she must conclude for herself that she has committed an error in judgment or action. Where I get myself into trouble is when I try to draw her error to her attention. The inevitable result of such an attempt is a painful reversal like the one described above.

And what is particularly impressive is how persuasively my wife can argue. Indeed, I'm convinced she could murder a neighbor and, with all the evidence pointing against her, still convince a judge, a jury, and even me that I committed the crime. "I did it judge, it was me, send me to the chair!"

In more recent years, I've come to realize that the real

reason my wife so successfully occupies the moral high ground in our relationship is that she generally does. It's a bummer, but it's true. The majority of our tiffs do result from my selfishness and insensitivity.

This realization consequently confirms one of my early lessons in marriage: the success of our marriage *does* largely depend on me. Fairness has no part in the marriage equation.

The minute I try to find the middle ground, I find myself slipping further and further into my own selfishness. Rather than reflect on my own actions, I obsess over my wife's, ceaselessly searching for the part she plays in the unfolding drama of our marital rumbles.

If I paid more attention to the part I play, I suspect there would be less rumbling and more tumbling in our marriage, if you get my drift. More important, in accepting the burden of my own actions as well as the responsibility for peace in our marriage, I suppose I'd ultimately find the balance in our relationship I expected to be there from day one.

Yes, herein lies one of the great paradoxes of marriage: by accepting responsibility, resisting the impulse to blame, and giving themselves totally and without reservation to their wives, men, I'm convinced, will find peace, balance, and fairness.

On the surface, my proposition hardly makes sense, I realize. But my experience suggests that selfishness elicits selfishness. Most fights between my wife and me gain momentum because I'm obsessed with defending my own interests, which in turn provokes my wife to defend hers. Remove my own self-interest from the equation, and the dynamics of the disagreement change drastically.

So my suggestion is to step to the plate and accept responsibility. I realize that this will require a leap of faith for many of us. It's not easy to withdraw from a full frontal assault, particularly when you fervently believe in the rightness of your position. But is your position really worth your wife's happiness or your peace of mind? Take the leap, and don't be surprised if your wife doesn't follow—that is, if she hasn't already leaped.

TWENTY-
eight

The Secret Life of the Bull Elk:
Plan a Family Vacation

I recently went elk hunting for the first time. I don't consider myself an avid hunter, nor do I fully identify with the guys on those hunting shows. You know the ones. Those guys with the thick southern drawl whose pinnacle of existence involves sitting in a tree stand in subfreezing temperatures waiting, sometimes for hours, for an unsuspecting prey. Those guys who, after killing their unsuspecting prey, approach the corpse of a creature they've just killed only to marvel at its beauty. "What a beautiful animal!" they exclaim, as if it's beauty could only be appreciated after the animal had been pierced by a 170-grain slug through the heart.

Don't get me wrong. I'm no environmentalist or animal rights activist. Like I said, I hunt. But I would like to think my motives for hunting differ slightly from those of the so-called sportsman. In fact, I take issue with any hunter who calls himself a sportsman. Hunting is hardly a sport. A sport implies competition between competitors. It suggests fair play. As soon as we arm the animals and allow them to shoot back, then we can call hunting a sport.

Nor do I revel in the thrill of the kill or litter the walls of my home with the stuffed remains of my trophies. Besides, the only room in the house my wife would allow a mounted animal to reside in is the garage.

No, hunting for me is a bit of a ritual that hearkens back to the primitive recesses of my being. The impulse to hunt derives from thousands of years of genetics. My earliest male ancestors hunted to provide for their families. Setting out from their caves with spears in hand in search of their prey, these men were driven by need. They were driven by pride. Their satisfaction derived not from the kill but from the knowledge that they'd achieved their objective. They had supplied their families with the necessaties of life—food and clothing.

Of course, I realize that providing for my family hardly requires me to hunt. For the money I dump into each hunting trip, I could certainly fill our freezer with store-bought meat. Nonetheless, stalking my prey, firing the perfect shot, and even gutting, skinning, and butchering my game makes me feel like a man in ways that pushing a shopping cart through the meat section of the grocery store can't. It tells me and my wife and children that I can put meat on the table.

And I enjoy the opportunity to study and admire nature. Take, for example, the mating habits of the bull elk. Once a year during what's known as *the rut*, bull elk round up a harem of cows, mate like mad for two or three weeks, and then head off into the woods until the next year. The beauty of the whole scenario is that the cows' hormones are raging at the same time as the bull's. I'm not even sure they mind that the bulls leave the rearing of the young calves entirely to them.

Imagine! The mature bull elk enjoys all the perks of marriage without any of the responsibility. He sows his oats once a year, turns his back on his harem, and goes off and does whatever he darn well pleases. No kids to tend, no wife to check in with.

On the surface, such an arrangement has appeal, I admit. As I sat on a ridge overlooking a bull surrounded by his cows, I couldn't help but envy the complete ease of his lifestyle. I imagined myself returning home once a year, mating like mad, and then heading off into the sunset. I would return the next year to see that the size of my family had increased by one and would repeat the process.

Then I realized that once a year would hardly cut it. The rest of the year would be one long, dark night of pent-up frustrations, culminating in a loss of hair and sanity.

I also realized that the responsibility I would be running from is, in many ways, my anchorage. It's what brings stability to my life. Where would I be without my wife reminding me that the toilet paper in the dispenser next to the toilet doesn't replace itself. I shuddered to imagine myself sitting for days staring at the empty roll, wondering when a new roll would spontaneously appear. My car keys would remain perpetually lost. I might even give up bathing. At a certain point, I would degenerate into a semicomatose figure seemingly attached to a recliner, mindlessly and methodically flipping from one channel to another. And then I would lose touch with reality, and my world would be reduced to a miniscule space that encompassed the kitchen, the bathroom, and the TV. Nothing and no one else would matter.

As admirable as the life of the bull elk might seem, our wives and children prevent us from descending into such a state. They provide the bulk of our motivation to be productive and responsible citizens. If the truth be told, the bull elk probably spends his year between mating searching for meaning that we men find in our relationships with our wives and kids. Besides, there's something to be said for year-round breeding.

Of course, some women probably believe that their husbands actually have much in common with the bull elk. These men mate like mad and leave the rearing of the children to them. All of us might do this to a degree. After all, bowling leagues weren't invented because men are especially fond of bowling. In reality, bowling is a lame sport, probably invented by men looking for an excuse to get out of the house one night or two a week. We might be more like the bull elk than we realize. We like the breeding part. It's the rearing that isn't always appealing.

One way of showing our wives that we aren't so bullish after all is to plan a family vacation entirely on our own. My experience indicates that women tend to instigate and plan most family vacations, and I know my wife would appreciate it if I took the initiative.

Of course, it's easy for me to plan a trip for just the two of us. Such a trip, like hunting, is another way to walk away from fatherly responsibilities and mate a bit. But planning a family trip shows our wives that we love them and want to share in the responsibilities associated with rearing a family. Better yet, plan the trip and make it a surprise. The kids will think you're especially cool if you plan a trip during the school year.

TWENTY-
nine

Growing Up
and Growing Down:
Rediscover Childhood Together

Realizing that I had to grow up was one of the most tragic moments of my life. Sure, my wife sometimes wonders whether such a moment actually occurred, but I assure you, it has.

It occurred one summer day on a trip to the local mall. I was on the threshold of adolescence, a time when *pimple* was the most harrowing word imaginable to my prepubescent mind. It was a time when I became painfully aware of my own awkwardness as I eagerly awaited the day when my head would grow into my unusually large ears.

It was under such psychological and emotional duress that a group of friends and I decided to ride our bikes to the mall. For the first time in my life, I would be making the trip without parental supervision, a sure sign that I was nearing manhood. I believed I would begin sprouting body hair any day!

But as I entered the mall, I realized that manhood came at a price: my friends and I strolled right past the toy store. None of my companions gave it a glance, and my body ached to veer in for just a moment. I could see kids, some no more than a month or two younger than myself, testing the remote-control cars. I wanted so badly to walk the action figure aisle.

I learned in that moment that boys on the verge of manhood had no business frequenting toy stores. Such a move was uncool, and I began to wonder if my own toys, the ones I had loved and played with my entire life, weren't responsible for my unusually large ears. Somehow, my infatuation with toys had stunted my growth toward adulthood.

The toys would have to go, all of them. Before long, my room was scraped clean of *Star Wars* figures and Hotwheels, replaced by cassette tapes and copies of *Sports Illustrated*. It was then, I convinced myself, that I started growing body hair.

In many ways, that trip to the mall was my rite of passage, but while I embraced the perks of adolescence—girls, a driver's license, and a midnight curfew—I never fully recovered from the loss of my childhood. For years I would stroll the mall, intentionally passing the toy store as many as a dozen times just to get a peek. I watched longingly from the sidelines as the toys I grew up with were resurrected for younger generations.

G. I. Joe made a comeback in the late '80s. The original *Star Wars* trilogy was digitally enhanced and rereleased; new and improved action figures soon followed, ones with moving joints! The new light sabers lit up and made sounds just like in the movies. They were like the toys I had grown up with, only better! The light saber I played with consisted of a long plastic tube attached to a flashlight. I was torn between my adult life and the childhood I had left behind. Trips to the mall became for me a living hell on earth.

And then, a miracle! My first child, a son, was born, and I was handed the excuse I needed. As a man, I couldn't go to the toy store; as a father, I had a moral obligation to do so, and our home has been littered with Hotwheels and action figures ever since. The difficulty now is convincing my wife that the toys we buy are actually for the boy.

She was a bit bewildered the first time she saw me sitting on the floor surrounded by army men while my son and I made machine gun sounds with our lips. "I'm just spending some quality time with my son," I sheepishly explained. She didn't buy it and one night asked, "Tell the truth, you like playing with Collin's toys, don't you?"

I couldn't deny it. Having toys in the house was like being born again, and with each of Collin's birthdays, things have just gotten better. We've moved from toddler toys into remote-control planes, electronic racing sets, and toy guns that fire actual projectiles!

Oh, that the boy would never grow up. But he will. He too will someday realize that toys aren't cool. I lament the day.

This experience has confirmed what my wife knew all along—men never really grow up. We're kids at heart.

But I'm also convinced that our wives aren't as grown up as they pretend to be. Most of them grew up playing with dolls, and while I have yet to catch my wife playing with one of our daughters' dolls, I'm not so sure our own kids haven't filled that role. When I was getting excited about buying Collin's first Tonka truck, my wife was eagerly planning and purchasing his first wardrobe. Overnight, Baby Gap became her favorite store, and I could hardly believe the outrageous amount of money we spent on clothes the kid would be lucky to wear for three months.

I was even more surprised to watch my wife dress and undress our first child a dozen or so times a day. "Look how cute," she gleefully exclaimed with each outfit. My wife was playing dress up. I kept thinking to myself, *And I'm the one who hasn't grown up?* Certainly this was proof that my wife hadn't completely abandoned her childhood. As it turns out, motherhood is actually an elaborate version of the girlhood game of house.

All this is to say that a little regression is good once and a while, and why not regress together? Go to the zoo, plan a trip to Disneyland or Sea World (without the kids). Spend an afternoon in a pet store, or go fly a kite. When the neighbors aren't watching, push each other on the swing, or take turns on the slide. Remember together how wonderful it was to be a kid.

thirty

The Shamu Principle:

Throw Her a Fish

Over the past few years I've developed what I refer to as the Shamu Principle, a highly sophisticated theory for promoting healthy relationships in any environment, particularly marriage.

Not surprisingly, my theory grew out of a trip to Sea World. The highlight of my trip was, as it is for most visitors, the Shamu show. I sat just out of splash range and was astonished as this whale, roughly the size of a small house, hurled itself into the air with the velocity and precision of a nuclear warhead launched from a submarine. Shamu would, on command, twist and turn, pull a back flip and then a front flip. Shamu even waved to the crowd on command, a feat parents spend months, oftentimes unsuccessfully, teaching their toddlers to perform. My own toddler has yet to wholly master the gesture. Shamu, a killer whale, waved with all the grace of a rodeo queen.

Indeed, Shamu did exactly what his trainers asked him to do. Not once did Shamu reveal even a hint of resentment or pent-up anger. I kept waiting, even hoping a little, for Shamu to suddenly turn on his trainers, perhaps biting off an arm as one of them fed him a fish. Or better yet, a full-fledged bloodfest with Shamu hurling himself into the crowd, viciously devouring a dozen or so bystanders. But nothing of the sort happened. Shamu flawlessly performed amazing trick after amazing trick, all for an occasional mackerel.

After the show, I couldn't help but approach one of the trainers. How in the name of Hades could they get an overgrown fish to perform with such precision? I couldn't even get my two-year-old to pee in the toilet.

Then came the explanation. When training Shamu, the trainers used only positive reinforcement. When Shamu performed well, they threw him a fish. When he screwed up, they threw him a fish. If he accidentally crushed a trainer while trying to jump through a hoop, they threw him a fish.

I was amazed. No electric shock treatment? No beatings? No withholding of meals? Just fish. Even if he failed, Shamu got a fish.

Then it occurred to me: if it works with whales, why not with humans? Though we pride ourselves on our superior intelligence, I began to wonder if we all aren't a little like Shamu, even my two-year-old. So my wife and I started throwing him fish. For just sitting on the toilet, pee or no pee, we gave him a treat. Even when he mistook the living room floor for the bathroom, we praised him for not soiling his pants. "Good job!" we exclaimed as we threw him a jellybean. We went so far as to carry a pouch full of treats at our hips, prepared at any moment to reward success or failure. And before long, he was peeing on his own, with a smile and a profound sense of satisfaction. It worked, the Shamu Principle really worked!

Spurred by our success, I considered to whom else I might toss an occasional fish. As a teacher, I naturally assumed that my students would be willing to perform for a salmon filet. Instead of merely criticizing their work, I emphasized the positive, and before long, they were smacking their hands together and *arfing* with great glee in anticipation of another fish. They developed greater enthusiasm for their work and my class, and they began to perform with the joy of a well-fed whale.

"What a revelation!" I thought to myself. By merely watching Shamu, I had discovered a means of influencing and motivating others. I felt a sudden rush of power, as if I could control the world and all things in it.

And then one night as I contemplated the uses to which I might put my newfound power, I made another telling discovery.

"Thanks for taking the garbage out last night," my wife said with a kiss, "I really appreciated it."

Without another word, I found myself hauling the day's garbage out into the garage. As I stood there looking into the abyss of the garbage can, I recognized that I had been victimized by the Shamu Principle. I had been thrown a fish and was immediately *arfing* with mouth wide open and begging for more.

Normally, I intensely resisted taking out the trash. My wife would ask, "Will you take out the trash please?" I would respond, "Yes, dear," and the garbage might sit for days until the stench got so bad that my wife took the trash out herself. I'm not sure exactly why I had such an aversion to disposing of garbage. I guess I never really saw it as a priority. It's not like the trash is going anywhere.

Even my wife's frequent complaints about my inability to fulfill that one husbandly duty did not produce the desired effect. In fact, after what I learned from Shamu, I'm not so sure that those frequent complaints didn't actually encourage the behavior they intended to criticize. I mean, there I was standing in the garage dumping garbage without having been asked or even nagged, and what was most perplexing is that I was, like my two-year-old, deeply satisfied with my performance. As I walked back into the house, I eagerly approached my wife and awaited my fish, and it came in the form of a kiss and another expression of gratitude.

As I returned to the TV and further contemplated the mysterious power of the Shamu Principle, I wondered why I so seldom threw my wife a fish. In reviewing my behavior, I realized that I was more likely to lob a complaint or well-aimed criticism in the direction of my wife than a fish. I had convinced myself that if I constantly reminded her how infrequently she surprised me in a sleek outfit or made the first move that she would develop an overwhelming desire to positively respond to my requests.

After several days of my not-so-subtle suggestions, I would arrive home from work expecting to see my wife in the glow of candlelight and clad in nothing but shrink-wrap. Or I would wait in bed, sometimes for hours, expecting my wife to roll over at any moment and make the first move.

But my complaints and less-than-subtle suggestions merely led to more complaints and less-than-subtle suggestions and no results. I daily returned from work to a wife frazzled by a day of intense motherhood, not shrink wrap, and I lost more than my share of sleep waiting for an eruption of feminine passion.

Could it be that my less-than-subtle suggestions were really a form of male nagging? Was it possible that I, a man, could nag? No wonder my wife wasn't responding. And if she ever did respond, would it be with the same resentment I carried with me to the garbage can after being pestered to death about taking out the trash?

No, I needed to start throwing her fish. What did I have to lose? Surely if they can get a whale to jump through hoops with a little positive reinforcement, I could get my wife to don a little plastic wrap. And as I changed my strategy, I came to understand why I had been so reluctant to throw my wife fish in the first place: criticizing is much easier, especially (and ironically) when interacting with the one you love the most.

Now each night as I take the garbage out, I ponder the real miracle of the Shamu Principle. If only more fish were thrown in every marriage, certainly we would see the divorce rate plummet. Eventually, my thoughts turn to my own marriage, and as I walk back in from the garage, I secretly hope to see the flicker of candlelight emanating from the bedroom.

Conclusion

While I have deliberately sought out the comedy in married life in the pages of this book, I hope I have made it clear that marriage is serious business. So much is at stake: our happiness, our wives' happiness, and the happiness of our children. With that said, I want to end on a serious note and suggest one more idea.

My mother unexpectedly passed away while I was writing this book. She would have been thrilled to see it in print with my name on the title page. All I can do now is imagine what might have been. I see her smile as she tells her friends and anyone who will listen about her son, the author. Like I said in a previous chapter, I was a mamma's boy for good reason.

And I can remember what it was like to have her in my life. Memories of my mother play like home movies in my mind, and these memories become more important with each passing day. One particular memory stands out as especially significant.

Each summer when I was a boy, we made our annual trip to Southern Utah as part of our summer vacation. My parents both have roots in Escalante, a tiny town not far from Bryce Canyon. Escalante is also the place where they met.

As we drove the scenic byways that lead to Escalante, my brothers and sister and I would marvel at the passing landscape of the high desert. We wondered how sand and rock could be as bright and colorful as a box of Crayola crayons. We pondered how wind and rain could carve bridges out of sandstone, and we would imagine that the clay spires and rock formations were spaceships and dinosaurs. And as we pulled into town, we waited. We knew from experience that it would come.

My father or mother would rehearse how they met, and we laughed as each recounted a slightly different version of the story. According to my dad, my mom made the first move; according to my mom, my dad did. They laughed with us and smiled at each other, and I saw a light in their eyes rekindle as they remembered together the joy of falling in love.

The story is important to me because it conveys in a profound way the love that served as the foundation of their relationship and our family. Their marriage was far from perfect, marked by little disagreements and marital tiffs. These disagreements were sometimes loud and occasionally ended in tears. As with most couples, the stresses of daily life took their toll on my parents and their relationship.

That's why the story of how they met was so important to all of us. It reminded my parents why they never gave up on each other, and it gave us kids a glimpse of something wonderful.

As I watched my father cling to my mother's hand as her

body rested in the casket the night of her viewing, I realized that their love survived all the disagreements and angry words; it has survived even death. What started as a mere crush in the small town of Escalante, Utah, became a resilient love.

Perhaps that's what ultimately distinguishes marriages that last from those that don't—a desire and commitment to love through both the good *and* the bad.

I think we all should rehearse from time to time how we met our wives and how we fell in love. And we should rehearse this story for our kids so they can see the exhilaration we felt in that moment. I would suggest writing this story down, presenting it to your wife, and someday giving copies to your children. Such stories should become a permanent part of your family record, something to be passed down from generation to generation. After all, is there a more significant event in life than falling in love with the woman you marry?

Index

About the Author

The son of an Air Force fighter pilot and a mother who believed he could do no wrong, Brett C. McInelly spent his childhood living throughout the United States and abroad. He was born in Wichita, Kansas, and spent time in Turkey, Germany, Florida, Washington, Virginia, and California before settling with his family in Farmington, Utah. After graduating from high school, he spent two years in South Korea before enrolling at Weber State University, where he earned a bachelor's degree in English in 1992.

While attending Weber State, he had the good fortune to meet Kristin Burnett, whom he fell in love with during their first date. Following a year-and-a-half courtship, the two were married in June 1993. They spent two years in Provo, Utah, while Brett worked on a master's degree in English at Brigham Young University. They then moved to Ohio, where Brett earned a Ph.D. in British literature at the University of Cincinnati. Brett credits his academic success to Kristin's unwavering support and encouragement.

Upon completing his degree, Brett accepted a position in 2000 to teach literature and composition at Brigham Young University, where he administrates the composition program. Brett and Kristin reside in Spanish Fork, Utah, with their five children—Collin, Katherine, Tess, Cosette, and Ethan. He enjoys golf, fly fishing, and a good story. Most of all, he enjoys spending time with his wife and kids, and navigating all the challenges and joys of married life. *Men and the Art of Marriage Maintenance* is his first book.

0 26575 08073 5